Credit Repair Secrets Learn Proven Steps To Fix And Boost Your Credit Score To 100 Points in 30 days Or Less

CREDIT REPAIR SECRETS LEARN PROVEN STEPS TO FIX AND BOOST YOUR CREDIT SCORE TO 100 POINTS IN 30 DAYS OR LESS

First edition. April 13, 2021.

ISBN: 979-8201483814

Written by Jake Robbins.

Table of Contents

Table of Contents
Introduction

1. How the Credit Score Work

What Determines Your Credit Score?
How Does a Credit Score Get Calculated?
The Impact of Bad Credit
Gaining Approval for a Loan Could Prove to Be Difficult

1. The Benefits of Good Credit

1. What Is Influencing My Score?

Where Do I Stand With My Credit Score?

1. 10 Ways to Positively Impact Your Credit Score

Tips to raise your credit score

1. Simple Steps to Correct Your Credit Score

Audit your credit reports.
Contest inaccurate late-installment sections.
Increment credit limits.
Open another credit card account.
Pay-to-Delete Strategy
Check for FDCPA (Fair Debt Collection Practices Act) Violations
Look for Errors on Your Credit Reports
Request Proof of the Original Debt

Pay the Original Creditor
Activate Auto-pay on Your Cards
Do Not Make Late Payments
Disputing Credit Report Errors
Contact The Offending Credit Bureau
Keep a record
Keep at it

1. How to Build a Credit Score From Scratch?

The first is to open a bank account
The second is to apply for a Secured Credit Card
Never exceed 30% of the credit card limit
Pay your installments regularly
Vary the types of debt as much as you can
Add your name to someone else's credit card as an "authorized user"
Download the free Credit Karma app
Negotiate Outstanding Balances
Pay Your Bills Twice Per Month
Increase Your Credit Limit

1. Start Repairing Credit Score

Credit Reports
Negative Remarks
Incorrect Entries
Increase Your Credit Limit
New Credit Card Accounts
Outstanding Balances
Compare the Interest Rates
Be an Add-On
Old Accounts

Timely Payments
Repay Student Loans
Automatic Payments

1. Credit Bureau and Credit Errors

How Do Credit Bureaus Gather the Information?
1. Information Supplied by Your Creditors
2. Purchased Information
3. Information from Other Credit Bureaus
What Are the Errors That You Should Check Out in Your Credit Report?
1. Personality Identity Information
2. Credit Account History
3. Credit Inquiries
4. Public Records
How Can You Get a Free Credit Report?
How Fast and How Many Points Will a Credit Score Improve
Realistic Time Frame for a Noticeable Improvement
What Impacts a Credit Report?
Why No One Can Guarantee an Increase in Points

1. How to Improve your Credit Score After Foreclosure and Bankruptcy

Managing Foreclosure/ Bankruptcy/Tax Lien and Other Judgments.
What is Foreclosure?
Now, Bankruptcy?
Types of Bankruptcy
Debt Discharge
The Payment Plan

Concerning business, the two types of bankruptcy are:
Reorganization Bankruptcy
Farming Bankruptcy
The Basic of Credit Card Debt and Bankruptcy
Know when short-term loans make more sense
Credit card debt can result in bad credit
Owing is the easy part, the hard part is paying credit cards back
You will find yourself spending more than you make
Most people use credit cards to handle emergencies
People think as long as they make the minimum payment they will be fine
Implications of Bankruptcy
Pros
Cons
So, what can you do to maintain it?
Building Not Activities Passivity
Keep in touch with credit institutions
Improve Credit Scores After Foreclosure
Improve post-foreclosure credit score
Guaranteed credit cards
FHA secured loans

1. How to Remove Mistakes from your Credit Report

How to Properly Dispute Negative Accounts

1. Credit Mistakes
2. Your Financial Freedom

What Is Meant by Financial Freedom?
Credit Cards and Financial Freedom - Is It Safe?

The Best Habits to Help You Reach and Protect Your Financial Freedom
Make a Budget
Set Up Automatic Savings Account
Keep Your Credit in Mind Without Obsessing Over It
It Is Fine to Live Below Your Means
Speak With a Financial Advisor
Completely Pay Off Your Credit Cards
Track Your Spending
Continue Your Education
Make Sure to Keep Your Mindset
Make Sure You Write down What Financial Freedom Means to You

Conclusion

Introduction

Do you know the implications of a credit score on your life? It might be a simple three-digit number, but it influences your life in ways you have probably never thought of. It determines your ability to obtain a new loan, purchase any assets, or even secure a job. Credit scores are usually calculated within the ranges of 300 to 850. The higher your credit score is, the better is your credibility. It essentially shows your creditworthiness. It indicates whether you are a worthy candidate for obtaining credit or not. Several financial agencies and institutions, along with landlords and even potential employers, use your credit score to determine your financial health. So, if you have a poor credit score, it is time to improve it.

The good news is you can repair your credit score. There are various factors which influence your credit score is like your payment history, utilization of credit, history of credit, diversity of credit you use, and the number of credit inquiries about you. Once you understand all these factors, you can take corrective action immediately. In this book, you will find all the information you need to get started with repairing your credit score. It will act as your guide on your journey towards a better credit score. You will learn about everything from understanding the basics of credit score, credit reporting, and the way credit reports are prepared to ways in which you can repair your credit score.

All the steps given in this book are practical and simple. You don't need to put in a lot of effort, but some effort is required. You can move from being neck-deep in debt to attaining financial independence you desire. If you're eager to learn more about all this, then let us get started without further ado.

1. How the Credit Score Work

There are quite a few specific factors that help determine a credit score. They are based on things an individual does or does not do with their available credit. This is why credit scores frequently change. We will be taking a more refined look at the variables that determine the credit score you end up with.

What Determines Your Credit Score?

The following are the five variables which determine a credit score:

a) Payment History - 35%

An individual's payment history is perhaps the most crucial variable used to determine a credit score. Lenders want to be able to know if the borrower can pay back the money they borrow. Payment history typically reflects every payment that has been made to service consumer debts. Lenders are required to report every time a payment is made to an individual's credit line, car loan, student loan, personal loan, cell phone contract, credit cards, and any other typical consumer debts. While almost everything is reflected in a credit report, mortgage payments are the exception.

Accounts are separated in the payment information. This payment information shows if you have or haven't made your payments on time, it also indicates if you are on a deferred payment plan. It also shows other information, such as payments that are not required at the moment, such as those for student loans, the number of payments made past due, the frequency of late payments, if a collection has been levied on your debts, and if there is a negative piece of information on your publicly available credit report. This information could be judgments, liens, or bankruptcy. Besides, the credit score reveals if any collection activities or late payments have been made. The great news is that older information tends to have less of an influence on your credit score.

b) How Much You Owe - 30%

Lenders take into account how much you already owe the moment you put in an application for credit. The payments you make currently actually help to determine if your budget can handle any additional payments for the extra money you want to borrow. While it is easy for you to believe that you can handle the additional credit, there is a chance, statistically speaking, that you won't be able to. Should you be close to the limit of a line of credit or about to max out your credit cards, you would signify to the lenders that you are a high-risk borrower. High risk, in this case, means there is an increased chance that you will be unable to maintain the payments.

This area of your credit score also reflects just how much you make use of the credit you have available on a regular basis. If you happen to use around 60% of your available limit on your credit card, your credit score could be negatively impacted. This is because if you were to lose your income source while owing a large sum of money, you could suffer difficulty in maintaining your payments.

c) Credit History Length - 15%

If you are the type of person that has had or made use of credit for an extended period, then your credit report can accurately reflect just how much credit you make use of, if you have any, and how you were able to get through a tough time. If you haven't used or had credit for quite a while, it can be challenging to ascertain whether you are a responsible credit user.

Regardless of whether the information is positive or negative, the majority of information is automatically removed from your credit report after a period of 6 to 7 years has elapsed. This means the only way to ensure that your credit report is active to make use of credit on a minimal yet consistent basis.

Only time can provide an accurate picture of just how responsible you are with credit, and that is why your credit history length is the 3rd most pertinent factor used to determine your credit score. This should accurately depict the first time you obtained credit, the period of time every item on your report has been reporting and if you are currently making use of credit.

Your credit score is likely to be poor if you are making use of credit for the first time. Being said, if you have been responsibly using credit over the years, this is bound to have a positive influence on your score. If you become involved in programs such as: consumer proposal, bankruptcy, debt management, or orderly debt payment, your credit history will be reset once those programs are completed.

d) New Credit Applications - 10%

When you frequently apply for new credit lines, you signal that you are in financial difficulty. The credit industry refers to this as credit shopping, and this is something that negatively affects your credit score. It isn't irrational for a lender to be concerned about the frequency at which you apply for new or additional credit. This is because the more credit you get, the harder it is for you to maintain every single one of your payments.

This aspect of the credit score considers the amount of times you have had your credit checked in a 5-year span, how many credit accounts have been recently opened by you, how long it has been since there was an inquiry on your credit and the amount of time that has elapsed since any new accounts were opened. This also takes into account if you are re-establishing your credit following prior payment issues.

e) Forms of Credit Used - 10%

This is the least significant variable used to determine your credit score, even though it makes up 10%. It, however, becomes important if you don't have much of any other information on your report. Varying forms of credit show an overall view of how you can handle money.

For instance, payment plans or deferred interest could indicate that you are not able to save for future purchases. Consolidation loans show that you found making payments for your debts difficult in the past. A line of credit is credit, the same way a credit card is a revolving type of credit, which means it is much easier to stumble using this form of credit than it is with an installment loan. If you concentrate on ensuring your finances are managed wisely, and you only apply for credit that you need, this of your credit score should sort itself out.

Other Variables

The variables stated above are calculated a bit differently by the major credit bureau organizations. The interpretation of these scores and the use of credit report information is typically up to every individual lender.

Apart from the variables listed above, there are other factors to consider when applying for credit. Banks and credit lenders will consider other variables like your assets, your income, the length of your employment, and your reason you are applying for credit.

How Does a Credit Score Get Calculated?

The agencies that report on credit collect a plethora of your personal and financial information to accurately calculate what your credit score is. This information can include:

· Personal information such as your occupation, address, and age;

· The sort of credit providers used by you in the past;

· How much credit you have borrowed before;

· The number of inquiries made about loan applications and credit applications;

· Overdue or unpaid credit or loans;

· Personal insolvency or debt agreements made relating to bankruptcy.

A credit score is typically expressed on a 0 to 1,200 scale, or even a 0 to 1,000 scale, however, this is dependent on the individual credit reporting agency.

The Impact of Bad Credit

The most popular way that creditworthiness is quantified is with the FICO score. It was developed by the Fair Isaac Corporation. A person's FICO score can be anything from 300 to 850. A higher score signifies that you are a lower credit risk.

Theoretically, there is no such thing as a bad FICO score; however, there is a chart developed by Experian that titles score range and breaks down the percentage of people in each group. Over 37% of eligible borrowers in the US have a credit score that is either fair or very poor. Less than 20% of eligible US borrowers have a score that is more than 800.

Having a credit score below 579, which is labeled as very poor, could stop you from possibly qualifying for either a line of credit or a loan. Having a score from 579 to 669 might require certain conditions like deposits or collateral before you can secure a loan.

There are, however, other scoring methods apart from FICO. Nevertheless, the metrics and principles used are similar. The truth is if your score is low using the FICO system, then it is probable that your score will be low any other metric, that being said, there are numerous ways to figure this out.

One method of learning your credit score is to put in a loan application. In the majority of cases, the bank will inform you of your score once you apply. Most people do not realize that they can request a copy of their credit report once a year for free. This report, however, does not include the FICO score. It is possible to request your FICO score for a fee.

Having covered this, let's delve further into some of the drawbacks of having a bad credit score.

Gaining Approval for a Loan Could Prove to Be Difficult

How good or bad your credit score is directly influencing your chances of being approved for credit or a loan. If your score is low, you are less likely to find a lender that is willing to give you credit. It doesn't even matter if your credit score is close to the bank's quality level or prime-subprime cutoff, most banks don't want to give loans to what they call subprime borrowers or individuals that do not meet certain criteria. While this can make you feel like the bank or financial institution in question is being unreasonable, numerous borrowers are affected by this. When you look at it objectively, having a credit score of 698 is not that different from a 702, however, if the 700 mark is an important one for the financial institution, those extra points can make a huge difference.

1. The Benefits of Good Credit

A person with a bad credit score can still obtain credit but may feel the consequences are too much. A poor credit score will result in high-interest rates that can quickly become expensive, especially if you take longer to pay your accounts. A good, excellent, or exceptional credit score will reduce the interest charges and help you to save money in the long run. There are many other benefits to having a good credit score.

Lower Interest Rates

Any person who has credit will need to pay interest on the outstanding account balance. The amount you borrow is often referred to as the capital balance. The balance outstanding is equal to the interest charges and the capital balance together. You can see interest as the profit the lending company gets for giving you credit; some places call it a financing cost. It is a fee that is levied every month in proportion to the amount of credit you have used and not yet paid back. A poor credit score will result in a higher interest rate and thus having to pay more fees. The advantage of a good credit score is a lower interest rate and pay fewer fees.

The lower interest cost makes it easier to pay back your capital balance. Most people are only paying back interest and then have the interest charged again on a monthly basis, which results in a vicious circle of only paying the interest. If you are only paying interest then it is difficult to pay back the capital balance you have borrowed. The better credit score and result in a lower interest rate can work to your advantage. It makes it possible to pay both interest and capital balance and in that way reduce your total debt.

Negotiating Possibilities

A high credit score provides leverage for negotiation. Your bank may have offered you a credit card with a set interest rate. You can approach other financial institutions and find out if they can give you a more favourable interest rate. This negotiating power helps you to find the best possible interest rate and offers with the lowest costs.

Having assets in your name will give you even more negotiating power. Lenders will always choose a customer who has security when it comes to providing credit facilities. Owning an apartment, vehicle, or other assets will give banks the knowledge that you can pay them back. Stable assets help in negotiations with financial institutions for decreasing interest rates and down payments. You should be proud of your high credit score and can always use it as leverage. Many people are scared to negotiate, but it can save you a bucket load of money in the long run. For example, an interest rate that is just 1% lower than the original quoted rate can reduce your total repayment with thousands of dollars. This money could be used in so many other ways than paying off a mortgage.

Improved Chance of Credit Approval

A better credit score makes it easier to be approved for further credit in the future. Every time you apply for credit, the financial institution will do a credit check. Your credit score is then made available to the company that made the request. The credit score will be used to help make a decision on whether the account should be opened, a credit card is issued, or a loan application approved.

Most people with a high credit score will qualify for a home loan or already have a home loan. Ensuring you make frequent payments on your mortgage can greatly contribute to a higher credit score, which will bring additional benefits. If you ever get to a point where you want to do renovations or need additional money, you can visit your home loan company and ask to refinance your home. This means that you will have funds made available to you but your mortgage will increase. You can still negotiate for good interest rates and lower fees. Plus, your long standing relationship with the lender makes it easier to approach them for additional financing.

Great Credit Card Offers

Financial institutions want to work with customers who pay their bills every month. Your credit score is one of the things that is appealing to banks. Many banks will pull credit score information to find potential clients. The bank will then contact you and offer you some great credit card deals. Your own bank is also likely to provide you with better credit terms. If you get a call from a financial institution offering to provide you with a beneficial credit card, then you are most likely doing a great job with keeping your credit score high. Listen to the offer and ask the contact person to send you more information via email. You can then check the options and decide if this credit card is a good idea.

A solid credit score will lead to offers of credit cards with good rewards and other benefits. Some lenders will provide a credit card account to you without charging any monthly fees. Other institutions have rewards programs linked to the credit card. Using your credit card responsibly and for certain transactions will give you points or a specific reward's level. A higher score will qualify you for more rewards. The rewards can include reduced prices on air-plane tickets or discounted rates on accommodation. Some financial institutions will add extra insurance cover, roadside assistance, or a personal banker to take your calls at any time of the day.

Better Insurance Rates

Car insurance is very important to protect you in the case of an accident, whether it is your fault or not. Automotive insurers look closely at credit scores when determining insurance premiums. The same goes for home owner's insurance. You need to have insurance to cover costs should your property ever sustain any damage. A person with a low credit score is perceived to be a high-risk client. The insurance company assumes that these people are more likely to claim from the insurance for unnecessary or fraudulent claims. This lack of trust results in higher insurance premiums.

A similar concept to the credit score is an insurance score used in some companies. The scores are not exactly the same but the general principle of a higher score is better stays the same. Your credit score will greatly influence your insurance score. People with a high credit score are seen as more trustworthy by the insurance companies. They benefit from lower insurance premiums thanks to a good credit record. Additionally, insurance claims may be paid more easily if you are in an accident or have damage to your home. After a claim, your insurance provider may increase the monthly premium to help cover some additional costs and to decrease risk. A higher credit score can be used to help negotiate a lower premium. Always ask your insurance provider to take your credit record into consideration when calculating your monthly premiums and excess amounts.

Better Rental Agreements

Landlords who rent out the property are always concerned about receiving their rental income. Many times a landlord will advertise an apartment but they don't know the people who eventually rent from them. Your credit score is one way for the landlord to learn more about prospective tenants. The landlord or rental agency will often use your credit report to see if you pay on time or miss payments. Often times, landlords are more willing to let property to people with a high credit score and will out rightly reject applicants with a low credit score. A person with a good credit score is more likely to be approved for renting property since the landlord knows that the person is likely to pay.

Landlords are more open to working with people who have a high credit score, which makes the rental relationship much easier. For example, a person with a high credit score may be able to negotiate for a lower security deposit, or even have the possibility of paying the security deposit over a two-month period rather than paying the full amount at once. On the flip side, a person with a low credit score will most likely be asked to pay a substantially higher security deposit.

Fewer Security Deposits

A security deposit is often requested by companies as it shows that you will pay your account in the future. If you do not make payments, then the credit provider can use the security deposit to recover some of the costs. Security deposits are used by companies that provide both products and services.

Cellphone companies often require a security deposit since the customer gets the phone before full payment has been received by the company. This situation is very risky for cellphone providers. The security deposit can cover some of the costs if a person stops paying their cellphone account. Other companies that may require a security deposit are those which offer utilities, such as gas and water. A person with a high credit score often has the benefit of not paying a security deposit or paying significantly less. Your credit history and credit score have proven that you pay your bills on time and provides peace of mind for the company.

Self-Confidence

> One of the biggest benefits of a good credit score is the boost your self-confidence experiences. You should be proud of yourself for saving your money and using your credit wisely. A good credit score takes time and effort to achieve. Achieving a high rating deserves a pat on the back. You also know that you can easily use your finances responsibly in the future.

1. What Is Influencing My Score?

The credit score or FICO score is a score that goes from approximately 300 to 850. That number is calculated using a secret mathematical formula where our behavior is taken into account when paying debts.

The credit score is used by banks, insurers, landlords, employers, companies, in general, to qualify us when they will give us credit, a job or even provide a service.

If my score is high, this tells the lender that I am a responsible person who has historically paid their bills on time. He/she feels calm lending me money because most likely he/she will pay it back.

If on the contrary, I have a bad score, the lender is running the risk that I will not pay him and lose his money. That's why he charges higher interest because apparently, I'm not so responsible with my debts.

Things that do not affect credit:

Building your credit history may not be easy, but it may be harder still to keep it clear.

A survey was recently conducted where they discovered that many people do not know what affects their credit score. For example, the survey revealed that:

- 63% of respondents believe that their income affects the credit score when in reality the income has nothing to do with the credit report.
- 60% of respondents think that work history affects the score. The work history does not influence the credit score at all.

▪ 53% of respondents think that the amount of savings and money in the bank is proportional to the credit score. Nothing is further from reality.

▪ 39% of respondents have the mistaken belief that age is a factor that influences credit scores.

Neither the income, nor the work history, nor the savings or the money that is kept in the bank, nor the age are factors that are used to calculate the credit score.

Factors that do, on the other hand:

▪ 35% of your score depends on your credit history: Or what is the same your debt history. If you do not have debts there is nothing to report, and if there is nothing to report then you have no credit history.

▪ 30% of the score is based on the debt levels: How much you owe in relation to the credit limit. Having credit and using a certain part of it does not affect your score, but if you have more than 30% of debts in relation to your credit limit, then you begin to affect your score negatively. If your debts go down too much, your score begins to disappear.

▪ 15% Time: For how long have you had credit. In other words, how long have you been in debt?

▪ 10% has to do with the type of debt: It is not the same to have a credit card of $ 500 that one with a limit of $ 25,000 or a financed car or a Lease. The more important the debt, the greater the positive impact on the credit score.

▪ 10% New applications: the last time you applied for the credit. Or what is the same the last time you applied to get into debt.

As you can see, the credit score only measures the capacity and fulfilment of debt payments.

Where Do I Stand With My Credit Score?

There are various ways in which one can look at what a good credit score is or is not. One of such is gauging an individual's credit score as this gives you the ability to properly estimate a borrower's capacity to pay back a loan. If the individual's score is high, this obviously entails that the person can be able to acquire valuable credit and also pay back the funds loaned to them in no time. However, if the score is low, the case is different. As for a low score, lenders will be very cautious of one who seeks a loan and it can be difficult for one to have funds given to them. To the lender's perspective, several scores have different meanings and deductions, based on which scoring system the creditor uses.

Obtaining the valuable credit score goes a long way to make a choice on if the funds should be loaned or not. This also helps these entities that want to extend credits to know the precise amount of money to give the person as well as with what interest rate.

Experian, Equifax, and TransUnion are the three most common credit reporting agencies. Each of these companies offers a free credit report individually making it a total of three reports per year. From this, you can tell that it is necessary that one reads and understands the contents that are on the report keenly. Information such as errors in the amount of monies to be paid back, payment histories and errors in late payment content can be seen. It also helps to confirm that there is no identity theft in the report.

Companies offering credit will be cautious in taking a closer look at numbers on the credit score of an individual. Lenders believe that a score of 700 or above is a very excellent one. One should value keeping their scores high at all times because there seem to be several advantages of obtaining a high credit number. Credit extensions having low-interest rate offers would definitely be secured by the high scoring report owners. Moreover, for those with high excellent scores, credit approval processes are normally done super-fast (in little or no time).

In the list below, a person can see, through a credit lender's eyes, the information and determine it:

v 760 or above:- Excellent

v 700 – 759:- Very good

v 680 – 699:- Good

v 620 – 679:- Fair

v 300 – 579:- Poor

Before applying for a big loan, it is important to note that the one who wants to credit is expected to screen their report at least up to six to twelve months approximately. Checking the report helps you see for yourself that the details are listed correctly and fish out errors that may not seem to tally. In a case where there are errors, the period earlier mentioned allows the one seeking credit to properly address the errors that may have occurred. In a case where errors on the report still surface at the time of applying for a large loan, it is still critical that the lender is made aware of these mistakes depending on the situation.

It is possible to improve on one's credit score. One of the ways this can be done is ensuring you pay all monies owed on a regular basis hence reducing your outstanding account balances. Since deadlines of payments are noted on every report, it is always best to pay in good time. For the borrower's sake, it would be advisable not to take on new debt.

To round this up, here are a few things I'll mention that point you to receiving a good credit score:

Speaking with creditors and credit advisors will be a major advantage for you as there are cases where one might be faced with a really terrible financial crisis where payments cannot be made within that time. The creditors would most likely be ready to assist to the best of their ability especially when it comes to lowering and spreading out payments.

Do not allow your credit card balances go to the roofs. Making them as low as possible is vital. I do not advise you to let them go high.

One thing that makes me laugh about some people is that they think they can improve their credit's score by simply just closing their old accounts so they hide late payments displayed on those accounts. It doesn't work that way. The late payment history will still show on the credit report even if that account is closed.

Lenders always check to see the credit history with active borrowing of last years or more.

Achieving a good credit score range might not be easy at first but it will go a long way to boost your personal financial life. All this must be done with a sense of keen insight as well as with careful thinking.

1. 10 Ways to Positively Impact Your Credit Score

The Recency Principle

When calculating your credit score, the most emphasis is placed on recent information. For example, a late payment one month ago has more effect on your score than a late payment a year ago. Therefore, time will gradually repair bad credit; every month that passes helps your score if you pay your bills on time. There are many ways to increase your credit score quickly, but the only way to increase it permanently is to pay your bills on time and let time heal any old wounds such as missed payments or bankruptcy.

Closing Accounts

One way to raise your credit score is by having three to five open credit card accounts, with each of them having very low balances. However, if you already have more than 5 credit cards, don't close any of your open accounts unless the terms are really bad (like a high annual fee). If the terms are bad, instead of closing the account, call the credit card company and ask them to waive your annual fee or give you a different card without an annual fee. Closing an account will lower your credit score by reducing your overall available credit and debt ratios. Therefore, only close your account as a last resort.

Collections

Late payments and collection accounts will significantly lower your credit score. Collections and charge-off are especially damaging. Even after a collection has been paid off with a zero balance, the fact that it is on your report will significantly lower your score for several years. Credit agencies don't look at your payment amount. All they care about is that your payments are on time or not, and how delinquent they were if not paid on time.

Delinquency Severity

Credit agencies measure in 30, 60 and 90 day increments. A 90-day delinquency is far worse than a 30-day delinquency and will lower your score accordingly.

This is why you have to understand how the system works! For example, late payments on a mortgage that are less than 30 days late are not reported. Therefore, it may be better to avoid paying your mortgage and pay your credit cards on time if you can pay the mortgage within that 30-day window. Utility companies do not report late payments, unless of course they turn you over to collections.

Getting An 800+ Credit Score

If you're going for perfect credit and want to maintain a score above 800, ideally you should have only three open accounts. But there are some specialized loans where you would need up to five open accounts with a reporting history of at least 24 months. Having a credit score in the 750 to 780 range is really excellent credit and will generally qualify you for the best rate on any mortgage loan.

Avoid the Credit Limit

High credit balances near the limit will lower your score once you missed a payment. Therefore, it is better to have several accounts with small balances than one or two accounts with large balances. You should maintain all your balances between 0% - 30% of the allowed limit for the best credit score. There is a modest hit to score at a 50% balance compared to the credit limit. There is a major hit to score at a

75% or higher balance. If balances are carried for some time at 75% or higher it will be impossible to maintain a credit score over 700.

Maxing Out

Any account that is maxed out repeatedly month after month will lower your score, even if you pay it off every month without being late or carrying a balance. The credit monitoring system will only recognize balances under 30% at the time your credit is pulled for the best score! The easiest solution is to get a credit limit raised and only borrow up to the 30% limit. Just call your credit card company and most of the time they will gladly raise your credit limit.

Payment History

Credit card payment history (revolving credit) has a heavier weighting on your credit score than installment loans. Therefore, it is better to pay down credit cards before paying down installment or auto loans.

Finance Company Loans

Having a finance company loan on your credit report will lower your credit score even if you pay on time. Having two finance company loans is worse; having three or more is worse still. A regular auto loan is not considered to be in this category. Beware of furniture companies, electronics companies, lumber yards and other companies who set up financing through a 3rd party finance company. These types of loans should only be used as a last resort as they will damage your credit while active even if you pay them on time.

Isolated Event vs. Habitual Offender

One isolated delinquent payment isn't very damaging, but frequent delinquent payments signals a red flag that you are a habitual late payer which will drastically lower your credit score. Also, sporadic late payments (a 30 day late last month and a 30 day late three months ago) are more damaging than successive late payments (successive 30 day late payments are called "a rolling 30" and it counts as only one late payment). This is because, if you're late multiple times in a row, agencies just assume you're going through a tough cash crunch. But if you're late and then on time and then late and then on time, it shows that you have poor financial habits and hurts your score even more.

Tips to raise your credit score

One simple way to improve your credit score is to lower your credit utilization. If you have a low credit limit, however, it can be difficult to keep your spending down 10% - 30% of this limit. Spending close to your limit, even if you pay it off each month, will not help your credit utilization. That's why it's useful to know how to increase your credit limit.

You could increase your overall credit limit by applying for more credit cards, but if you have a few already, it may be better to ask your creditor if they would be willing to increase the limit. If you have been paying in full every month, and have build up a good relationship with your credit card company, they may be willing to help you. This allows you to increase your credit without the hassle of opening new cards and having additional credit inquiries.

The following are some tips for getting your credit score increased:

Don't Ask Too Soon

In most cases, your credit card company is going to automatically check your credit about six months after you opened the account to see how things are going and they may increase your credit at this point. If they do not, however, it's fine to call them and ask them to increase it. You should never ask for an increase before waiting at least six month.

Don't Ask For Too Much

You should be conservative when you ask for a credit increase. It's not a good idea to ask for double or triple your current limit. If you ask for too much, it's likely the credit card company will decline and then you will have to wait some time before asking again. It's best to ask for no more than a 25% increase at one time.

Use Your Card Often

A good way to show the issuer that you deserve more credit is to use your card on a regular basis and pay it in full. This may mean putting a larger balance on the card and then paying it back over a few months. This shows your creditor that you need access to more funds, but that you are still responsible enough to handle larger limits responsibly. The easiest way to do this is to stop paying for things using cash. Instead, put everything you can on your credit card. This allows you to build up a strong history of paying off large balances each month.

Limit Requests

It's not a good idea to ask for limit increases for all your cards at once. This is because each time you make a request, your issuer is going to make a credit inquiry. If the issuer sees a few hits on your report at once, especially from other credit card companies, they will see this as a big red flag. Instead, limit your request to your best credit card company. It is better to make a strong case to just one company, rather than spreading yourself out and trying to convince a bunch of companies. If you do get denied, wait a few months before trying with a different issuer.

1. Simple Steps to Correct Your Credit Score

Improving your credit score can mean qualifying for lower financing costs and better terms. That is genuine whether you need a decent credit score to acquire cash for personal reasons or so you can buy stock, rent an office, etc. to begin or develop your business.

The issue is that a credit fix is similar to improving your expert system: you consider it when it is essential. However, if you don't have excellent credit, it's almost painful to address that circumstance short-term.

That is the reason an opportunity to begin fixing your credit is currently - before you genuinely need it.

Luckily, it's not too difficult to improve your credit score.

Here's the recommended procedure you can follow.

Audit your credit reports.

The credit authorities - TransUnion, Equifax, and Experian - are required to give you a free duplicate of your report once every year. You should simply inquire. (Snap your connections to demand a copy.)

Another approach to see your credit reports is to utilize free assistance like Credit Karma. (I'm not supporting Credit Karma. I do like it and believe it's convenient. However, I'm an individual who believes other free administrations are similarly valuable.)

When you've joined, you can see your credit scores and view the data contained in the reports. As a rule, the passages on the different stories will be the equivalent, however not generally. For an assortment of reasons, credit reports are infrequently indistinguishable.

Contest inaccurate late-installment sections.

Errors occur. Your home loan bank may report an installment was late which was in actuality paid on schedule. You can contest late installments regardless of whether accounts or records have been shut, similarly to how you debate deprecatory imprints.

Increment credit limits.

Another factor that weighs intensely on your credit score is your credit card usage: The proportion of accessible credit to the credit utilized has a significant effect. As a rule, conveying a parity of in excess of 50 percent of your affordable loan will contrarily affect your score. Maxing out on your cards will hurt your score.

Open another credit card account.

Another approach to expand your credit card usage proportion is to open another record. For whatever length of time that you don't convey an equalization on that card, your accessible credit quickly increments by that card's breaking point.

Attempt to get a card that doesn't charge a yearly expense. Your most solid option is through a bank where you as of now have a record. Without a doubt, cards with no annual payment will in general charge higher loan fees. However, if you never convey an equalization, the financing cost is unessential.

Pay-to-Delete Strategy

If you have derogatory items in your credit report, you can opt to pay the unpaid credit balance only if the creditor agrees to delete the items from your credit report. This method works through the idea that your report doesn't show whether you have had any history of bad credit in the derogatory items section. This will ultimately improve your rating. Actually, the idea is to ensure that whatever amount you agree to pay doesn't show up as the date of the previous activity. If the creditor only cares about their money, why should they bother telling the world that you have finally paid?

In most instances, the creditors often write off debts within just two years of constant defaulting, after which this information is sold in bulk to a collection company for pennies. This means that the collection companies will be just fine even if you even pay a fraction of what you ought to pay. Whatever you pay, they will still make money! This makes them open to negotiations such as "pay to delete" since they have nothing to lose anyway.

Therefore, only use the pay-to-delete approach at this level and not at any other time. Actually, the only other way around it for the collection company is a judgment, which can be costly, so you have some advantage here.

Additionally, use this strategy when new negative items start showing up in your report that could hurt your reputation as a credit consumer.

Check for FDCPA (Fair Debt Collection Practices Act) Violations

The law is very clear on what collection agencies can do and what they cannot do as far as debt collection is concerned. For instance:

- They should not call you more than once in a day unless they can prove that it was accidentally dialed by their automated systems.
- They cannot call you before 8:00 a.m. or after 9 00 p.m.
- They cannot threaten, belittle, or yell at you in an effort to make you pay any outstanding debts.
- They cannot tell anyone else other than your spouse why they are contacting you.

- The best way to go about this is to let them know that you are recording all their calls.

- They cannot take more money from your account than you have authorized if they do an ACH.

- They are also not allowed to send you collection letters if you have already sent them a cease and desist order.

Look for Errors on Your Credit Reports

Your credit report should be free of errors. Even the slightest thing as reporting the wrong date of the last activity on your credit report is enough to damage your credit. Your last date of activity has a profound effect on your credit rating. If the write-off date is different from what has been reported, you can dispute the entry to have it corrected to reflect the actual status of your credit. However, keep in mind that the credit bureaus will, in most instances, confirm that the negative entry is correct even if this is not the case, which means that they will not remove the erroneous item.

Request Proof of the Original Debt

If you are certain that the credit card has been written off for late payment, it is highly likely that the carriers (Capital One and Citibank) cannot find the original billing statements within 30 days, which they are required by the law to respond with. This, in effect, allows you to have whatever entry you have disputed removed from the credit report as if it never happened.

Pay the Original Creditor

When your debt is sold to collection agencies, you will probably risk having new items showing up on your credit report, which can further hurt your credit rating. However, you can stop that by sending a check with the full payment of any outstanding amount to the original creditor, after which you just send the proof of payment to that collection agency or any other, and then request them to delete any derogatory items they have reported on your credit report.

Activate Auto-pay on Your Cards

It does not matter if you make use of an actual calendar stuck to your wall or if you use your smartphone's app to set an alert, you should do whatever you can to be reminded when payments on your credit cards have to be made. Ensure that you try to pay more than the minimum consistently. When you take into account that the most significant determinants of your credit score are your payment history and the size of your debt, it makes sense to pay as much as you possibly can towards your debt.

Do Not Make Late Payments

You should try to avoid missing payments or even contesting them, as this could damage your score. If you have missed payments in a period of 3 to 5 months, your account could be closed by your lender. When this happens, it is referred to as a default. Defaults get recorded in your credit report and they not only lower your score, but also make it more difficult for you to gain credit down the line. A default stays on your record for 6 years. The only way it does not appear is if it was recorded in error.

Disputing Credit Report Errors

If after reviewing each credit report, you find a high priority credit error, what's next? You need to take action and get those errors deleted or corrected as quickly as possible. Begin by writing the offending credit bureau and the creditor directly. See the Appendix called "Credit Dispute Letter" for an example of a dispute letter and the Appendix called "How To Get Your Free Credit Report" and "Identity Theft: How To Report It" for credit bureau contact information. Be sure your letter specifies the error and be specific in how the error needs to be corrected. Request a letter to be mailed to you that confirms that the action has been taken.

Disputing an error with a credit bureau or creditor is free. Once you formally contact them, they will investigate the disputed claim and, if applicable, delete or correct the error. The following three steps are recommended when disputing an error with the credit bureaus.

Contact The Offending Credit Bureau

It is possible that not all creditors report to all the credit bureaus. For this reason, only contact the credit bureau that is reporting the erroneous negative credit information.

Use the "Credit Report Dispute Letter—Sample" in the Appendix.

Explain in your letter what is inaccurate and give specific directions as to the corrective action you want to be taken.

When possible, include proof in your letter to support the claim.

Enclose a copy of the credit report, with the item(s) in question encircled. (Make sure to send the credit report to the corresponding credit bureau.)

Within 30 days, the credit bureau is supposed to confirm with the creditor and investigate the disputed information.

The creditor is required by law to investigate the disputed data and report its findings.

If the dispute results in a change to your credit report, the credit bureau will send you a written response and a free copy of your updated credit report.

However, if the creditor disagrees with your claim, the credit bureau will mail you a written explanation stating the disputed item is accurate.

Keep a record

Keep records of all phone and email communications.

Keep copies of every letter sent and received.

Keep proof supporting your claim — this can include anything from canceled payment checks to past billing statements.

If you're missing key billing statements, the Fair Credit Billing Act requires each creditor to keep past statements on file which you can request for a fee.

Call the creditors' billing or record department, and ask for what you need.

Keep at it

Continue to check your credit reports at least once every 12 months. Make sure no new derogatory or harmful errors or negative information has been added to your credit report, and ensure the corrected errors have not been included in your credit record.

1. How to Build a Credit Score From Scratch?

There are several ways and all of them are effective.

The first is to open a bank account

Having an account open in itself will not increase your score, but it will give you a starting point to show regular income. After a few months, you can ask your bank (remember to show off your best smile) what services they offer to increase your Credit Score. My bank, for example, offers a mini loan of $ 500 tied up to be returned in 6 months. It means that you deposit $ 500, they re-loan them to you at a favorable rate and when, in 6 months, you finish paying the installments, they give you back the $ 500. Practically in 6 months, you paid interest as a "tax" with the sole purpose of accumulating points. To put it in simpler words: from 500 and 500 you return, then you pay 500 in installments + interest and you return 500 at the end. It is an expense, but this type of loan guarantees you a considerable accumulation of points, but only if you are regular in payments.

The second is to apply for a Secured Credit Card

Unlike traditional credit cards, you do not have to show any kind of entry to get approval, but you also have a usage limit. The only thing required is a deposit which is returned to you after a year of regular use. Until a couple of years ago, the deposit was around 200 euros, but with the debt problems that developed after the recession, all the major credit companies have lowered the costs. For example, I applied with Capital One (but there are many others like Discover). The deposit was only $ 49, and the card limit was $ 200 a month with the option of

2% cash back on gas or restaurant expenses. I started using it regularly every month ONLY for these two things and, after a year, my Credit Score was already considered very good, they also returned the deposit and the cash back and the credit limit rose to 500 dollars after only six months. Of course you are not obliged to use it only for these things, but I have limited myself for two reasons.

The first is to accumulate cash back (i.e. a refund) at the end of the year. The second is to make sure I never use more than 30% of the card limit. Which brings me to the next point.

Never exceed 30% of the credit card limit

Believe it or not, it is essential that you show that you do not need a credit card to pay for your things, but that you use it only when strictly necessary or as an optional choice.

The more you use it constantly the better, but judiciously.

Pay your installments regularly

All the above points have absolutely no value if you are not constant in payments. No one here scales your loan or credit card debts from your salary. It is your responsibility to remember when you have to pay or set up an automatic payment from your bank account. I decided to set up automatic payments.

Even if your memory is excellent, you never know what can happen that can distract you and cause you to forget the due date. So I strongly suggest you do the same because even one missed payment will negatively affect your score.

Vary the types of debt as much as you can

If you can make the Secured Card And the mini loan with the bank at the same time, do it. The more options you have, the faster your Credit Score will grow. Of course, always keep in mind that if you don't pay on time, this will have the exact opposite effect and your credit score will plummet before it even had a chance to grow. So if you're not sure you can do better, don't risk it and wait a little longer.

Add your name to someone else's credit card as an "authorized user"

If, for example, you are married to an American who has had more time than you to accumulate a decent score (as in my case), it might be a good idea for him to indicate you as an authorized user of his credit cards. This does not mean that you will actually have to use his credit cards, but the more his score improves, the more he will positively influence yours. Be careful though! If you go down, he comes down with you. This type of choice involves a large demonstration of trust so be careful not to betray it.

Download the free Credit Karma app

Not only does it constantly give you a detailed report of your score, but also what has positively or negatively influenced it, which credit cards or loans are best suited to your situation, your progress, and many other functions. It's all free and, although not updated to the minute, rather accurate. It does not lower your Credit Score and also offers you many other services such as online and free tax returns. Due to Credit Karma, other major credit companies have also had to adjust to offer the Credit Score free check. For example, Capital One and Discover have now integrated this service into their offers (although in a more limited way).

If you follow these tips in a year you can afford to ask for a car loan without having to pay disproportionate interest or even more, depending on your income and your general receivables/payables situation. This reminds me of how important it is to start as soon as possible. Remember that this is the first thing they look at when you need to apply for a loan!

How to Grow a Good Credit Score Over Time

Once you've begun to climb your way out a bad credit score, the most important factor then becomes growing your score. Of course, making your payments on time is a great way to balance your previously negative activity, but there are other, more creative ways in which you can achieve this same result.

Let's take a look at the ways in which you can grow your credit in the eyes of a lender.

Negotiate Outstanding Balances

Let's say that you have a debt that ultimately had to go to a collection agency because you refused to pay the debt back within a timely manner. Of course, the debt that you owe is going to reveal itself as a negative on your credit report, but if a collection agency is involved you have the opportunity to change somewhat the way in which this debt is perceived. This requires negotiation skills. By going to the collection agency and negotiating a deal where you only end up paying a portion of your debt instead of the full amount, you look responsible. Additionally, your credit report will show that your outstanding debt has been settled, and this will help to improve your score. Other tips include making sure to put the agreement in writing, stating exactly how much you are agreeing to pay.

Pay Your Bills Twice Per Month

Let's say that you've had a particularly grueling month in terms of unanticipated bills and expenses. To compensate for this, you've decided to spend close to your credit limit. Your credit limit is four thousand dollars, and this month you have already spent three thousand. This situation is not the worst for you, because you know that you have the funds and are planning to pay off the full amount of your debt by the end of the month. Instead, you should consider making multiple payments throughout the month. This way, you will be able to reduce the amount of debt that the credit card company sees. It will seem more like you simply reallocated your funds in a certain way, instead of making it seem like you are maxing out a card and are having trouble financially. This tactic should especially be considered if you own other credit cards that are close to being maxed out or are maxed out in their entirety.

Increase Your Credit Limit

If you are not in the position to paydown high outstanding balances that exist on your credit cards currently at this time, another good option is to request an increase on your credit limit. Especially if you have recently gotten a raise, this could be a great option for you. As we discussed before, having low utilization is key to maintaining a good credit score. By opening up more credit for yourself, it looks like you are using less credit compared to the current credit that is available to you. While this will serve to grow your credit successfully, it can be risky if your spending habits are less than conservative.

You need to make sure that you're not going to immediately spend more of your credit once the credit company has extended it for you. If you have a feeling that this might be a result of a credit extension, seek out one of the other options that were presented in this chapter. Similar to a gambling addiction, sometimes it can seem like spending credit card money creates a thrill because the necessity to pay back the funds is not immediate. If you are finding that you have a hard time resisting the urge to spend large amount of money on your credit card, you might have a credit card addiction. If you notice that you are frequently maxing out your credit card on purchases that are frivolous or unnecessary, you may need to seek help. Even if you don't see yourself as a complete credit card addict, seeking financial counseling might help you save money. Saving money can also help grow your credit score because the money that you save is money that is not being spent in ways in which cannot be paid back. To put it more broadly, learning how to be financially responsible will help you to grow your credit. Knowing what to save and how to save it, as well as learning how to properly manage your funds are techniques that can be aided by hiring a financial advisor.

1. Start Repairing Credit Score

You will have the power to negotiate for lower rates of interest if you have a good credit score. So, to do this, you must start repairing your credit score. The tricky part is that repairing your credit score is quite similar to improving your professional network. You tend to think about it only when it matters. However, you cannot improve your credit score overnight, and it takes time, consistent effort, and patience. So, start working on repairing your credit right now instead of waiting until you really need to repair it. In this section, you will learn about a couple of ways in which you can start repairing your credit.

Credit Reports

You merely need to request a copy of the free credit report you are entitled to from each of the three credit rating agencies in the US. Apart from this, you can also use a third-party service like Credit Karma to view your credit score. The credit reports might not always show the same information. So, before you can start to improve your credit score, you must review your credit report.

Negative Remarks

If you want to dispute any errors or entries in your credit report, you have to write letters to the concerned credit bureaus. These days, you can raise a dispute online and don't have to go through the hassle of writing letters. Ensure that you don't ignore any discrepancies in your credit report since they can ding your credit score. If you notice any wrong information about a collection account, raise a dispute. For instance, let us assume that you filed for an insurance claim for major surgery. The insurer claims your claim was paid whereas the health care providers claim that they haven't received any payments. In such instances, your account can end up with a collection agency, and the same will show up on your credit report. This is a miscommunication that can cost you dearly. So, if you notice any such discrepancies, get it fixed immediately. Once the dispute is resolved, the incorrect entry will be removed from your credit report.

Incorrect Entries

Everyone makes mistakes. There might be times when you made a timely payment, but it was wrongly reported as late payment by your mortgage lender. A credit card company might fail to report a timely payment. Whenever you notice such incorrect entries, you must dispute them the same way you dispute any negative remarks. Your payment history accounts for a considerable chunk of your credit score. So, any incorrect entries about late payments can ding your credit score. This is one of the main reasons why you must keep reviewing your credit reports periodically.

Increase Your Credit Limit

Your credit utilization ratio matters a lot while calculating your credit score. Credit utilization essentially refers to the ratio of the credit you use against the total credit available to you. Usually, it is a good idea to ensure that the balance is at least 30% while using your available credit. If you start maxing out your credit cards, it will certainly harm your credit score. By paying down your balances, you can improve the credit utilization ratio. Another tactic that can be easily used is to increase your credit limit. If the outstanding amount due on a credit card is $2500 and the available credit limit is $5000, you can significantly improve your credit utilization ratio by increasing the credit limit to $7500. Even if your expenditure stays the same, when the available limit increases, it makes it seem like you have more funds at your disposal. When it comes to calculating your credit score, it is all about relativity.

You will need to put in a requisition for the increase of your credit limit with your credit card provider. Usually, most of the credit companies will be more than happy to comply with such requests. However, while doing this, make sure you don't increase your expenditure as your credit limit increases. If this happens, it will merely defeat the purpose. You must try to reduce your debt and not sink more into it.

New Credit Card Accounts

Another simple tactic that you can use for improving your credit card utilization ratio is by adding new credit accounts to the existing ones. This technique works pretty much the way the previous one does. While doing so, ensure that you don't carry any balance on the new card that you add to your credit portfolio. While opting for a new credit card, check any annual fees that are applicable or payable by you. You are trying to merely increase your credit limit and not trying to incur additional expenses. Keep this in mind. There are certain issuers who expect you to make a minimum transactional amount on the card that you take and charge exorbitantly high rates of interest on the same. So, carefully go through the terms and conditions of service before you avail a service. The interest rate will be irrelevant if you don't plan on using the card much. Also, don't make too many inquiries about several new credit cards within a couple of months. Multiple inquiries about this will be counted as a hard inquiry and will reflect in your credit report. If the number of hard inquiries increases, it will render this technique useless.

Outstanding Balances

You will need to start paying down on any outstanding balances you have. I know this doesn't seem like a logical thing to do, especially when you're trying to improve your credit score to obtain more funds. Still, I urge you to start decreasing the available outstanding balance to improve your credit score. It might mean that you need to start budgeting your monthly expenses. Living frugally for a while might also work. Paying down balances might not be easy, especially in the short run, but it is an essential part of your long-term financial strategy. Over time, your credit score will increase while the interest that you are paying will decrease. By doing this, you are essentially saving yourself some money.

Compare the Interest Rates

When it comes to your credit report, the age of credit is important. Whereas, when it comes to your bank account, interest rates matter. If you are $100 per month toward paying down balances, then concentrate on paying off loans that have a higher rate of interest. Start prioritizing all your debts according to the interest rate payable. For instance, if you have a credit card debt of about $5000 payable at 19% interest, it is a better idea to clear this credit card debt before clearing dues on any other card you used. Also, take into consideration the principal owed. At times, clearing off small loans can give you the motivation required to keep going. You will need to spend some time and crunch a few numbers before you can conclusively prioritize your repayment strategy.

Be an Add-On

As previously mentioned, if you are an authorized user on someone else's credit card, the primary user's credit history will affect your credit score. So, it is a good idea to ask someone you trust to add you as an authorized user for their credit cards. For instance, if your partner has a credit card with minimum balance and a good track record of payments, it will be helpful for your credit report if you are an add-on to such a card. On the downside, if the primary user keeps making any late payments or defaults on any payments, it will harm your credit score.

Old Accounts

If you have a credit card, which has been with you for a long time, then don't surrender it. Regardless of whether you actively transact using it or not, it helps improve your credit score. It is directly related to the age of your credit history. For instance, if you have a credit card, which is over ten years old, then closing it will merely harm your credit score. If you want, you can always apply for a new card, but don't get rid of the old one.

Timely Payments

Missing out on even one payment will severely damage your score, especially if you are trying to improve it. If there comes a situation where you are able to pay all your bills on time, you must start being smart about it and check if any of the bills can be paid at a later date. For instance, any late payment will be reported by the lender who provides your mortgage or even a credit card company, but certain late payments on utility bills will not be reported until four months like the cable bill. However, I suggest that it is always a good idea to make timely payments whenever possible. By doing this, you not only save yourself from a lot of unnecessary stress, but even your bank account will be thankful to you.

Repay Student Loans

If you have any student loans, consider repaying such debt as quickly as you can. The longer the debt stays unpaid, the more interest will you end up paying. Did you know that student debt in the US accounts for over $1 trillion? If you want to improve your credit score, repay the student loans. You might be making monthly minimum payments on the student loans you have. If you increase the repayment amount, you can reduce your student debt. For instance, divert any windfall gains or extra earnings towards the repayment of student debt. Let us assume that your student loans account for $25,000 payable at an interest of 10% for ten years. Now, if you start increasing your monthly repayment by even $150, you can repay the entire loan within five years. By doing this, you can save a lot of money which might have been directed towards unnecessary interest.

You also have the option of repaying your student loan in two installments every month. If you are paying $500 every month, make sure that you pay $250 at the beginning and the rest towards the end of the month. If you make a repayment once every two weeks, you will end up making 13 repayments in a year. So, you are effectively making one extra payment per annum. This also helps to reduce the total amount outstanding as you student debt. Also, when you make two payments, it reduces the financial strain you feel. Apart from this, you can also automate the payment of student debt. By doing this, you can effectively reduce any chances of missing any payments and ensure that all the installments are paid on time.

Another option available to you is to refinance your student debt. You can do this if you have a steady stream of monthly income. If you have $50,000 as student loan payable at 8.5% interest per annum, you can perhaps refinance it with a personal loan at a lower interest rate. If the loan you took out for refinancing is payable at 4.5% interest per annum, you can save on the interest payments you make.

Automatic Payments

Any monthly bills or utility payments can be set up for automatic payments. To avoid missing out on a payment or making any late payments, automate certain recurring payments. As long as you have the necessary funds in your account, you can use automatic payments for improving your credit score. Timely payments can help improve your overall credit score and reduce the likelihood of paying any late fees.

When you automate certain fixed monthly expenses, it helps you set up an effective monthly budget. By budgeting your expenses, you can prevent yourself from going overboard. If your monthly expenditure is $2000 and you spend $1000 of this towards payment of utilities, you will be left with $1000 to spare. You can even set up standing instructions for certain payments. If you know you have to $1000 every month toward utilities, set it up for autopay. By doing this, you can improve your ratio of credit utilization.

If you are working on improving your credit score, then keep track of all the payments you make. Try to stay on top of all your payments and avoid making any late payments while repairing your credit score.

1. Credit Bureau and Credit Errors

How Do Credit Bureaus Gather the Information?

1. Information Supplied by Your Creditors

Usually, without your consent, your creditors send your credit information to credit bureaus. These records are sent in a format that you don't have to know. But the essential content is the personal information with which you got the loan, the type of loan it is, the terms and conditions, and how well you have played it by the book.

Of course, it is not a dark market, so you are expected to know that they send this information to credit bureaus. It is only ironic that these same credit bureaus pay to access the information.

2. Purchased Information

By legal standards, some information isn't accessible to the public. They are considered confidential, not illegal. Due to the legitimacy of credit bureaus, they often access such information, but as you guess, they part with some dough in turn. This sort of information mostly contains public records, judgments, et cetera. You can be sure credit bureaus are not interested in your personal life, adventures, or such data that are not relevant to your credits, not even your entire finances.

3. Information from Other Credit Bureaus

Despite being competitors, credit bureaus are mandated to share information sometimes. Not all the time, since each one paid to obtain their data. But sensitive data about your credits are exchanged. For example, one updates the others the instant a fraud alert was raised, or attempts were made to hack your credit report, etc.

There it is! You now understand how consumer reporting agencies gather your data and how it is being used. The next thing we should be talking about is the errors that can be found on your credit report. But before that, you should meet three major credit bureaus.

You need to have some idea who you are getting your credit reports from. Right? Entirely logical. Let's latch onto that then.

What Are the Errors That You Should Check Out in Your Credit Report?

1. Personality Identity Information

Any slack can lead to errors. So, your full name should be spelled and arranged correctly. The same thing about your Social Security Number. How about your address? Your date of birth too. For instance, if you have earlier raised a fraud alert, security freeze, statement of dispute, etc. Whatsoever you have raised earlier, and you find documented, be sure that is exactly what you have here.

2. Credit Account History

This is the most essential part of the whole credit report, as we have earlier disclosed. You may want to pay close attention to every detail provided here, from the reports of lenders on the transaction you have had with them, to the type of transaction stated that you have had.

You also want to check their reports on the agreed duration, the duration you paid, your credit limit, your payment pattern, history, et cetera. Data as simple as account name and number should be doubly verified.

I'll be quick to add that a leak is possible from anywhere, your credit union, credit card issuer, or your credit bureau themselves.

3. Credit Inquiries

Only creditors to whom you apply for a loan can automatically request your report. The list of the inquirers and the type of credit you're hoping to have with them are displayed here.

You want to make sure that a stranger or an unknown company hasn't woken up one day to start gathering data on your credits. The moment you find one of those, you have got something to fix on your credit.

4. Public Records

To cap this, you need to scan through your public records too. We know that bad records don't help anyone, and it can't be exciting to find strange ones in your report.

If one of your credit records is overdue for removal, there is no reason you should still have it there. For the records that are still to be reflected, you want to make sure they are not understated or exaggerated. Inconsistency and inaccuracy can give you a bad light in front of every creditor.

There we are! You have just taken a tour of the Credit Bureaus and the errors you may pick out on your credit report. With that last lesson in mind, let's see about fixing your credit reports!

How Can You Get a Free Credit Report?

If you are reading this from any other part of the world, I hate to say you'd have to consult something else. Perhaps your government service, a credit officer, or anything. But if you are wondering how to do it in the U.S., it is laid on the lines here.

You need to remember that if you are checking a similar site and not exactly this, you may be charged at some point, or worst, you might be playing into a fraudster's net.

Right after filling in the personal data, pick your preferred credit report (whether Equifax, Experian, or Trans Union). On the next display, you verify your identity by answering a few questions that are directly related to your credit history. Then, your credit report is displayed on the screen.

You can simply print or return to view. Right-on. If this is not, consider calling 1-877-322-8228 and go through a similar process over the phone. You'd have to wait for a couple of weeks or one more before receiving your credit report.

♦♦♦♦

Check Out Your
Credit Report

How Fast and How Many Points Will a Credit Score Improve

Realistic Time Frame for a Noticeable Improvement

As mentioned, there are many steps you can take to improve your credit score. By paying off any credit card debt, disputing any errors in the report, or by even paying off any collection accounts, you can significantly improve your credit score. You must take steps to increase the positive information, reduce the negative impact, or a combination of the two in the credit report.

By doing this, you can start seeing an improvement in your credit score within a couple of weeks. For instance, by doing something as simple as making monthly payments on time, you can improve your credit score. It would help if you did this consistently, as it isn't a one-time thing. You can see an improvement in your credit score within weeks, but for a significant change, that will take a couple of months at least. Here are three factors that define the time frame for improving your credit score:

The First Factor Is the Starting Point

It takes at least a month to develop your credit score on your own. If you are trying to repair your credit, then it will take longer. For instance, if you are eligible only for a secured credit card and have damaged credit, then it can take anywhere between 12 and 18 months to improve the credit score.

The time frame will depend on how responsibly you use the approved card. The amount of pre-existing negative and positive information in your credit report will also influence this time frame.

The Second Factor Relates to the Punctuality of Your Monthly Payments

Your credit score depends on the compilation of information in the credit report. To repair damaged credit, you must keep adding positive information to the report every month. It means that you must pay all your bills, including any credit card bills or monthly repayment of a loan on time.

If you do this consistently for a couple of months, it will improve your credit rating. Also, if you have a credit card, try not to max it and instead use it wisely. Maintaining a healthy level of utilization can add positive points to your credit score.

The Third Factor Is to Define What Improvement Means to You

You will start to see your credit rate improving by a few points in a couple of weeks while it takes a couple of months to see your score change from bad to good. So, your perception of what improvement means matters while repairing your damaged credit.

At times, a minor mistake like maxing out the credit card limit or missing a payment can damage your credit. Some might be trying to recover from things they didn't realize could harm their credit like applying for a new credit card or closing an account.

Others might be dealing with more significant issues like bankruptcy. Depending on the reason that led to the depreciation of their credit rating, the time taken to get back on track will vary.

You might not have realized it, but whenever you apply for a new line of credit or close an existing account, it reduces your credit rating. The damage in such instances is minor, and the recovery time is around three months. Some major issues severely damage your credit ratings like defaulting on payments and bankruptcy.

The average recovery time for bankruptcy is over six years. You can fix the damage from defaulting on payment within two years. Then there are moderate issues like maxing out the credit card and the recovery time for these issues is three months or more.

These are just examples of how long it can take and isn't a precise estimate. The period of recovery also depends on the other information present on the credit report. Apart from this, the amount of positive and negative information on the credit report influences the recovery time. If you have a solid credit history, then it is easier to fix a misstep.

However, if your credit report is riddled with mistakes, it will become quite challenging to repair. The lower your credit score, the lesser ground you have to cover, and the easier it is to improve the score.

For instance, A and B have both defaulted on their mortgage payments. A has a credit score of 780, while B's credit score is only 680. A will take anywhere between 3 and 7 years to repair the score while B can repair it within ten months. Improving your credit score isn't a one-time thing, it is a continuous process.

The addition of information to the credit report will keep altering the credit score. Your financial goals, along with your existing financial position, are two factors that influence your need to improve the credit score.

What Impacts a Credit Report?

From a lender's perspective, the following points are positive items on a credit report:

- If you pay your bills on time and do so consistently.

- Have been and still can maintain a reasonable balance of unused credit.

- Apply for credit only when the need arises. When you do this, the number of inquiries against you is to a bare minimum.

- Consistently check your annual credit reports and correct any mistakes in them.

- Certain red flags that a potential lender looks for in a borrower's credit report include the following.

As you can see, different factors influence your credit score. Every financial transaction that you make impacts your annual credit report.

Paying your monthly cable bill might be a small transaction, but it does affect your credit report.

If you consistently pay your monthly utility bills, it will help improve your credit score. However, if you get behind on payments or miss due dates on monthly utility bills, then it will significantly decrease your credit score. If your credit score is less than 579, then you will be viewed as a risky borrower by the lenders. A score of 582 to 669 might qualify you for approval of loans from some vendors.

A good credit score is between 670 and 739. You are a dependable borrower if your score is higher than 740. You qualify as an exceptional borrower if your credit score is more than 800.

Why No One Can Guarantee an Increase in Points

As mentioned earlier, your credit score is a three-digit number. Not just banks and lenders, but several other companies have also started using credit score as a measure of your ability to repay a debt. Equifax, Trans Union, and Experian are the three main credit bureaus that create all the credit reports. Vantage Score and The Fair Isaac Co-operation (FICO) are credit scoring models that then use the information given in the credit reports for coming up with an individual's credit score. The credit score is usually in the range of 300 to 850.

The credit bureaus might also, at times, generate credit scores based on some other proprietary model. The credit score is calculated based on different things like the frequency of payments, duration of the accounts, or the expenditure you incur, and so on. Credit scores aren't influenced by personal demographics like sex, age, religion, nationality, or marital status.

There are different ways in which credit scores are calculated, and therefore, it is not unusual to have multiple scores simultaneously. Your credit scores depend on the bureau or the agencies that the specific lender reports. For instance, a lender might report to two agencies.

You can have multiple credit scores if a lender doesn't report to all three agencies at the same time. Apart from this, the lending situation can also mean that you have different scores. For instance, the credit model used by a mortgage lender will be different from that used by other lenders.

Regardless of the model used, these scores are based on all the information present in the credit report.

However, the formula that is used for obtaining these credit scores is closely guarded much like the fried chicken recipe at KFC or the formula used in Coca-Cola. Certain factors have a positive or negative influence on your credit rating. If you look at all the information that is available online, you will notice that you can certainly improve your credit rating by following specific steps. The one thing that no one guarantees is the number of points that are associated with each factor that influences the credit score.

It is safe to assume that not paying your cable bill for six months will hurt your credit score. However, it isn't possible to estimate the number of points you will lose when you get behind on your payments.

This estimation isn't possible because the formula used for calculating the score is safely guarded. Apart from this, the effect that a specific factor has on one's credit score also depends on their existing credit score.

1. How to Improve your Credit Score After Foreclosure and Bankruptcy

Managing Foreclosure/ Bankruptcy/Tax Lien and Other Judgments.

First, what are the public records you can expect on your credit profile? Three kinds of horrible public records used to be displayed on a credit record. But not anymore. You may have heard and wild guesses about this, but straight from the horse's mouth, only one kind of public record is displayed in a credit report: Bankruptcy. But before we jump into that, you need to know that bankruptcy, even though it is the only record displayed on your profile, is not the only one to worry about. Foreclosure is equally crucial. We will start with that, and then we will see how to handle the records on your profile. Here we go:

What is Foreclosure?

Foreclosure is used to describe an official situation where a lender takes control of the asset which was indicated as collateral while applying for a loan. This means foreclosure occurs when a debtor takes over property or assets to sell when the lender doesn't pay back the money borrowed.

Though foreclosure does nothing on your credit profile, you obviously need to avoid it at all costs. Whatever you used as collateral must be something of considerable value to you. Probably your house (mortgage), your parcels of land, or a vehicle you need for work or family duties. It hurts to see those things go.

Foreclosure is a long and arduous process too. It may span up to 700 days. So, even lenders try to avoid it if they can. Foreclosure usually takes place in different formats. Some are called Judicial, others Non-Judicial. The fundamental difference is that judicial foreclosure requires the lender to obtain official consent from the court before auctioning the property or seizing it. In Non-Judicial cases, the lender is not required to obtain court permissions. They can simply seize their assets.

Just like every other loan, the easiest way to avoid foreclosure is to pay your loans on time.

Now, Bankruptcy?

Bankruptcy is a financial declaration that a person is no longer capable of paying the debts he has acquired. It is a court proven declaration that a debtor has exhausted all means of getting the funds they owed and failed. And now, all creditors will have to be lenient with them. In some way, it sounds like a method of getting relief from your debts, if not all, some.

The introduction of bankruptcy laws came after a long time when lenders could be stigmatized for life, forced into slavery or pash them down to their children.

In our days, when you declared bankruptcy, you are required to declare all of your assets. For example, if you declare bankruptcy with an outstanding of $80,000 you will state all of your personal items and assets from your house, including chairs, dresses, and artwork. It is then the job of the creditor to decide whether some of those items hold value, and can be sold, seized or not. As it turns out, many people often lose more than they were hoping to when they declare bankruptcy, and it becomes a win-win situation for creditors.

Debtors of course realize this before it's too late. This is why many attempt to mess with the records and give false statements or declarations to conceal their assets. These acts are considered Bankruptcy Fraud and are heavily frowned upon in the US. If you are declaring bankruptcy, be set to face the full complications.

Bankruptcy is filed in a situation where a debtor declares that she is entirely incapable of paying further loans. She has tried all other methods, and she is left with no choice than to seek leniency from the court.

When this is approved, the debtor declares the total assets and they are liquidated, in other words, sold to cover whatever it could of the loans. Afterward, the debtor is completely absolved of further payments. The only problem is that it reflects on your credit score for ten consecutive years. This means that every potential creditor can understand that you have been in a financial mess at some point, and you had to give things which do not measure up to the value of the loan. That is never a good sign, and singularly, it will be the reason you might not be able to get a loan for the first years after.

Bankruptcy is declared in situations where a debtor is confident that he could pay the debts but considering his current financial situation, they would need a long period to pay. This time could span into several years. In the end, a repayment plan is approved by the court, and the debtor pays over that period. He is absolved of the debt after payments. Bankruptcy reflects on your credit report for seven years. It faces a lot of criticism, and it could be a reason you're turned down too, but less likely.

Only an organization or individual that is unable to completely honor its financial obligation or make payment to its creditor files for bankruptcy. This goes to say that a bankruptcy filing is a legal course of action taken by a company or person to relieve themselves from debt obligations where all outstanding debt of the company is evaluated and paid from the company's assets. As legal proceeding goes, bankruptcy is carried out to give individuals and businesses freedom from debt they have already incurred and at the same time provide creditors with the opportunity to get their debts paid. It can be said to allow for a fresh start by forgiving debts that cannot be paid and at the same time offering creditors a substantive opportunity to get methods of repayment based on the available assets of a person or business that can be liquidated.

Theoretically, this can mean that the ability to file for bankruptcy can benefit a whole economy by giving businesses and individuals a second chance to have the utmost access to consumer credit and by providing creditors with a reliable measure of debt repayment. Once the bankruptcy proceeding is successfully completed, the debtor is to be relieved of their obligation from the debt that has been incurred before filing for bankruptcy. However, it will be on their credit record that such a person has acquired debts before and filed for bankruptcy. This information is going to remain on the record for about seven to ten years depending on the type of bankruptcy filed.

Types of Bankruptcy

There are two types of bankruptcy.

Debt Discharge

This is simply the cancellation of debt, thanks to bankruptcy. Based on the Internal Revenue Code, a debtor must add into their gross income, the discharge of indebtedness after which a court must have discharged his/her debt upon meeting all conditions.

However, if a debtor should refuse financial counseling, commits a crime, fail to fully explain the loss of his/her assets, provide false information during court proceedings or basically disobey the orders of the court, a judge can rightfully refuse to discharge the debt of such a person.

The Payment Plan

This is a kind of bankruptcy filed, where a debtor and his/her lawyer submit to the court, a kind of repayment plan of how the debtor plans to pay off his/her debts in three to five years. This plan is dependent on the debtor's income, food, and utilities, tax, and healthcare expenses.

Should the court approve the plan, the debtor proceeds to make the payments required as stipulated in the plan. If such a debtor is consistent with the payments, the remaining debts at the end of the three to five-year period will be discharged. The payments are made to a trustee from the bankruptcy court that then proceeds to pay the creditors while getting a commission too.

Concerning business, the two types of bankruptcy are:

Reorganization Bankruptcy

This is a kind of bankruptcy filed which is meant to help business owners who have serious issues with their business but still have regular income and valuable assets, reorganize the business. The business is allowed to continue its operations with the court's supervision of course.

The creditors aren't allowed to interfere with the debtors during the supervision. Business owners will have to share their reorganization plan with the creditors and provide them with part of the payment. But if the creditors do not agree with the plan, they have the right to file a competing plan.

Farming Bankruptcy

It is a type of bankruptcy specially designed for farmers of the same family. It is to help the family reorganize their farming business as well as settle all their debts.

The unpredictable nature of farming and seasonal trends are factors that are seriously considered.

The Basic of Credit Card Debt and Bankruptcy

People know the basics about credit cards. Once you are approved, you then receive your card and activate it. You can use it for pretty much anything, such as for purchasing groceries, clothing, or for paying bills.

The nice part is that you only have to make the minimum payment every month to keep yourself out of credit card debt. Unfortunately, it is this kind of thinking that often leads people into credit card debt.

Below are some basic points that most people don't realize about credit card debt.

Know when short-term loans make more sense

Sometimes we need to get some cash or find a way to pay a few bills quickly. Many people turn to credit cards for these reasons. They receive their approval within minutes and their card will arrive in the mail in about five to seven business days. However, sometimes it is better to go to your bank and talk to a loan advisor instead. If you need a couple thousand dollars to pay off your medical bills so they aren't sent to a collection agency, it might be best to take out a short-term loan from your local bank or credit union.

Credit card debt can result in bad credit

Paying off your credit cards in a less than a timely manner or missing the minimum payment aren't the only things that are going to result in your having bad credit; having credit cards that hold high balances can also increase your chances of bad credit. This is why it is important never to max out your credit cards. You should make sure you always have at least 30 percent of your credit limit available.

While it is almost impossible in today's world, your best chance of keeping yourself from having bad credit is by remaining as free of debt as you possibly can.

Owing is the easy part, the hard part is paying credit cards back

The reality of life is that you never really know what is going to happen. You could have a job for a couple of decades and then find out that you are randomly laid off due to cutbacks. You could have an illness spike that causes surgery.

There are a lot of situations that can cause you to miss credit card payments and not be able to cover your bills.

You could also find yourself struggling to pay the full minimum balance, so you may decide to pay about half of it every month.

You will find yourself spending more than you make

It doesn't matter how responsible you are with credit cards; one of the biggest reasons people find themselves in credit card debt is because they spend more than they make every month.

Credit cards are very tempting because they provide you with the thought that you can just pay it back later or make smaller payments on the purchase every month.

Although, in reality, you should never spend more than what your monthly income is.

Most people use credit cards to handle emergencies

It is common for people to tell others that a credit card is only used for emergencies, but do you keep in mind what a true emergency is? Most people live paycheck to paycheck. Therefore, when they see their checking account balance drop low and there are several days before their next payday, they will start to think about each purchase they make and wonder if they should use their credit card as it is considered an emergency or a need. The best step for you to take is to start slowly saving a part of your check and place it into an emergency fund account.

People think as long as they make the minimum payment they will be fine

In reality, you always want to make sure you pay more than the minimum payment. Think of it this way: if you have a $75 minimum payment, at least 25 percent of what you pay is going to go toward interest and fees. This means that you are only putting 75 percent of your payment toward paying off your debt. Depending on how you much you owe, this could be a low amount. If you aren't careful, you could find yourself going over your credit limit, which means your credit card company will charge you their over-the-limit fee.

Furthermore, only paying the minimum payment is going to take you years to pay off. It really doesn't matter how low you feel your credit limit is versus how high you believe your minimum monthly payment is. It can still take at least a couple of years to pay off your debt, providing you stop using your credit card.

Implications of Bankruptcy

Before you consider filing for bankruptcy, you first need to understand how it works as well as the pros and cons. It's not a simple issue that can be done quickly but has a complex side only a bankruptcy attorney understands. It would be best if you find out everything you can before filing for bankruptcy. Find below the consequences of filing a bankruptcy.

Pros

Discharge: Getting debts discharged is one major reason people file for bankruptcy. And when such debt is discharged, erasing all your debts as well as preventing creditors from collecting further payments from you, the debtor becomes relieved. It's one huge advantage of filing for bankruptcy. Not everyone who filed for debt discharge is granted. If you owe debts on alimony, tax liabilities or child support, filing for bankruptcy would be a waste of time. Such debts are not forgiven nor discharged.

Automatic Stay: Here is another advantage to be enjoyed when a bankruptcy is filed. It is a situation whereby the person who files for bankruptcy becomes automatically protected from the creditors, as well as the property over the collection of debts. The protection stays until the court finally decrees the debts to be honored and forgiven or discharged. In a situation that involves divorce proceedings, the automatic stay might be lifted.

Cons

Loss of Property: There's a possibility that a bankruptcy filer might lose his property if the court decides it's valuable enough to pay off the debt owed. This would happen if you include your property in your case to the bankruptcy trustee. Your creditor would have higher leverage in trying to get your property especially if you used such property initially as collateral.

Credit Score: Another downside to filing for bankruptcy is that it decreases your credit score. Loaners will only see you as risky when they check your credit history because filing for bankruptcy won't in any way clean up your debt history even though your debt is canceled. However, it's a better option than acquiring debt. You can always rebuild your credit score later.

Privacy: If you're sensitive about your privacy, filing for bankruptcy might not be for you, and this explains why you must do your research if you want to file for bankruptcy.

You can either prepare yourself against the consequences or look for other options. When you file a bankruptcy case, every detail about your financial statements becomes public. In other words, anyone can access your personal information without your permission. The amount you owed, who your creditors were, and your bankruptcy schedule can be assessed easily by anyone. This can be quite a bid deal if you value your privacy.

So, what can you do to maintain it?

Prevention has always been better than cure. But if you are here already, it doesn't help to keep musing over the error you've made. Pick yourself up and be set to make a better impression in future endeavors.

Try to pay other debts promptly. The more you perform better in other debts, the higher your chances of weakening the effects of bankruptcy on your profile.

Building Not Activities Passivity

This may not be explicitly mentioned anywhere, but it is just common sense. Increasing assets increases reliability. If you have sufficient resources, you will be able to mortgage them for credit. So creditors will give you credit for getting a good guarantee in exchange for their risk.

Avoid construction liabilities like credit card bills as it will affect your rating negatively.

Keep in touch with credit institutions

Always be truthful about your financial situation and be in good terms with them. Always keep in touch with them and express your inability to pay, if that is the case, and see if it is possible to make an agreement in any way. After all, they want their money and not the rating to fall.

Improve Credit Scores After Foreclosure

Foreclosure can drop a consumer's credit scores with a huge margin. If you have had the misfortune of going through a foreclosure, then the following article will tell you how to rebuild your credit score.

A fall in house prices, the subsequent recession, and the high unemployment rate has caused a number of people to default on their mortgage payments. Bankruptcies and foreclosures followed as a result of defaulting on capital and interest on home loans. Since the consumer payment history is one of the most important factors affecting the calculation of credit scores, a foreclosure obviously had a negative impact on the credit rating of all those that lost their houses. Hence, the topic of improving credit scores after the foreclosure has taken on great significance.

A creditor can initiate the foreclosure procedure and complete the entire process outside the court system, assuming that the mortgage deed has a sales clause power. In the absence of a sales clause power, the lender has no choice but to take the borrower to court. In other words, judicial foreclosure is expected. Regardless of the nature of the proceedings, the details are listed in the public record and the consumer's credit report. The information remains firmly positioned in the consumer's credit report for a period of 7 years. As mentioned above, the consumer's credit score decreases from 350 to 400 points following a foreclosure sale. Although a spotted credit report and a low credit score is a double whammy, a number of creditors give proper credit to the consumer's efforts to improve credit scores. Good credit scores are a must to procure loans at a favorable interest rate, for availing insurance, and for the sake of applying for jobs that require the applicant to assume managerial and financial responsibilities.

Improve post-foreclosure credit score

In order to improve credit scores after foreclosure, you should avail either installment or revolving credit and make it a practice to pay interest on a regular basis. Establishing a history of regular payments can go a long way in helping the consumer build his / her credit scores. The same approach can be adopted by a consumer who is interested in improving credit scores after bankruptcy.

Guaranteed credit cards

People can opt for secured credit cards to rebuild credit since consumers can be approved for these cards within 6 months of a foreclosure sale or discharge failure. These credit cards are guaranteed by a CD which acts as a guarantee for credit card companies. The credit line is usually 50 to 100% of the deposit amount. A practice of repaying the entire balance on the credit card on a monthly basis will result in the credit card company extending further credit lines to the consumer without further deposits as collateral. A secured credit card is converted into an unsecured credit card within 18 months, assuming that the consumer is careful with payments.

FHA secured loans

People whose homes have been foreclosed are required to wait for 3 years from the date of a foreclosure sale to avail themselves of an FHA insured loan. Assuming that the consumer is approved for a secured credit card and brings his / her credit score up to 620 points, FHA secured loans can become the springboard for further improvement in credit scores. The Federal Housing Administration (FHA) offers secured government mortgages that protect the lender in the event that the homeowner's default values on the mortgage. Thus, the consumer can take advantage of a down mortgage by paying only 3.5 percent of the home purchase price.

These measures are not only useful for consumers who are interested in improving credit scores after foreclosure, but also essential for people who are eager to improve their credit rating after debt settlement since a debt settlement does not completely cancel out information from the consumer credit report. The net result is a good credit report and satisfactory credit scores.

Anytime you apply for one of these services with bad credit, you end up paying a deposit. This makes moving into a new place more expensive because you need deposits for all your bills. Fixing your credit means a higher credit score, which can help you avoid these deposits.

1. How to Remove Mistakes from your Credit Report

Now, if you have an outstanding balance on your cards take a moment to write it down. List each card that currently has a balance, how much the balance is and how much is late. This may seem depressing when you look at the amount of debt that you have but it's important to understand. Some of the smaller debts may be possible to get rid of quickly if you're careful and you think it through. Some of the larger ones you may be able to work with pretty well at the same time.

Consider what your income is and what money you have available to spend towards your debts. Do you have enough that you could pay off a few of the smaller debts and still leave a couple of credit cards open? If you do that's great. What you want to do is call up the company and negotiate with them. Offer them a smaller amount than what is owed and tell them that if they are willing to accept that amount you can pay them immediately. Most credit card companies will jump at the offer. Even if you offer them $100 or more, less than what is actually owed, they will be perfectly happy taking the money because they know it's at least going to get them something. On the other hand, if they refuse there's no telling if you'll declare bankruptcy and then they will never get their money.

Paying off the cards will effectively close them because your credit granting company is going to take the card away from you as soon as they get their money. That's why you don't actually want to pay off all the cards that you have debt with. If you pay them all off then you're going to lose every one of them and that's going to result in no new credit being added to your credit report. That's actually going to hurt you even more than it's going to help. It may seem strange since you're looking at debt (which hurts your credit) but if you close out those accounts it's actually going to be worse than if you keep that debt hanging around at least a little while longer.

What you need to do is start making payments. Even if you owe a lot of money to a credit card company or a loan company they will rarely close the account or turn it over to a collections agency if you are making payments. They'll wait until you stop paying because, at the moment at least, they can expect to get their full amount back. If they sell the account to a collection agency they will get only a small percentage of the actual amount owed from the company. By making payments on time you increase your credit score because the algorithm that's used to calculate on time payments doesn't consider whether the actual amount due is past due. All it focuses on is whether the payment is made by the due date.

When you continue making those on time payments you also have credit. If you have credit this also counts in your favor. If you close those accounts you lose the open credit that you have and your credit score will actually go down (even though you've gotten rid of debt). So, make sure you keep those cards open and don't completely pay off the amount that's owed. Once you get the balance to a level that you can manage continue to make additional purchases and pay them. This is going to build your good credit even faster.

Once you've managed to pay the outstanding debt your credit company is less likely to pull your card away as quickly because you will still have new charges to pay off and they now have a little more trust that you're going to pay it back to them. They will likely allow you to keep the card and that's going to increase your ability to build credit. Having the open credit and then having a low minimum balance on the cards will increase your score by a lot.

What a low balance means is that you make sure not to spend a lot of money on your credit cards and you keep the balance low. When you open credit cards you are given a limit. That's the amount of money that you are allowed to spend on that card. When you keep the balance (the amount you have spent) at the low end of this limit it actually improves your credit score. When it's high your credit score tends to go down. But you don't have to be careful about each credit card (though that's the best way to do it).

All of your credit cards are added together in order to create your total balance. So if you have three credit cards for $1,000, $1,500 and $500 your total available credit is $3,000. If your $500 credit card is completely maxed out but you haven't spent anything on the others then your credit score is still going to be pretty good because your total balance is about 16% of your available credit. On the other hand, if you had maxed out the most expensive card your credit used would be about 50% and this is not going to look so good on your credit score.

In order to improve your bad credit, it's important to pay attention to your balances. Try to keep them down and try to make payments on them frequently. This is going to help you develop a track record for trustworthiness and that's going to ensure that other credit companies are willing to give you credit and willing to let you keep that credit as well. If at all possible you want to make sure that this happens because the only way to build your credit is through having credit. Just getting rid of the debt isn't going to do enough.

Finally, if you don't have credit cards open right now you want to get them. You want to have at least three cards that have revolving credit. That means you want three credit cards that you are using and making timely payments on. If you do this, it's going to help you improve your score even as you work towards fixing some of your other problems. These new cards may have to be secured because the company does not trust your credit score and believes you will default on the money that may or may not be owed to them.

Make sure that you get the credit. Take small credit cards with secured amounts and make sure that you pay them on time. If you do this it's going to boost your score. You will definitely be surprised how quickly those positive ratings will start to show up as well. Just take advantage of them and keep building your credit.

Most people who are regarded as a bad credit risk is likely to be shut out by the same society, which flourishes on credit. You may find this such a huge contradiction. Being marked as having a bad credit may result in having deep internal wounds. This is because, naturally, you would not want your neighbors to find out about your bad credit. Worse, it would be a dishonor on your part if your entire community would found out and be the topic of their gossips.

In truth, however, you do not have to deal with this type of mentality even if you have a bad credit situation. This issue is only a result of exaggeration from federal authorities and financial institutions that almost 40% to 45% of the people are in a bad credit situation. Consequently, when you are considered as a bad credit risk, the doors that were previously open would most likely be closed, which is one of the downsides of bad credit. Bad credit only implies that future financial institutions will be careful when carrying out transactions with you. For instance, you may be obliged to pay earlier than you used to, which is to be expected. Besides, if you were in the shoes of these financial institutions, you would also do the same.

If you are already in a situation of bad credit, it is best to use real money when purchasing instead of plastic, such as credit cards. This can help you spend less and you will be inclined to avoid even the most effective marketing strategies of companies. You need to get a hold of yourself by learning the techniques and tools on how you can cope with your bad credit situation. The key is to fight the situation in order to restore your good financial state as well as your dignity.

How to Properly Dispute Negative Accounts

You'll be able to monitor if someone ever steals your identity and you're also going to be able to keep track of the accounts that are affecting your credit score both in positive and negative ways.

If you look at your credit report and see a lot of negative accounts, such as past due or collection accounts, consider whether they are accurate. What this means to you is that, if the negative accounts on your credit report are not 100% accurate you can request to have them removed. What you want to do is review your report and consider which accounts may not be correct. Now keep in mind you're not allowed to dispute anything that is true. Sometimes they will continue to tell you an account has been verified when you know it isn't accurate. If this happens you'll have to go above their heads and write to the original creditor, letting them know that the account is inaccurate and providing information that verifies this. This could be statements showing your bills were paid on time or letters indicating that they removed the account. Remember to send copies of these documents and not the actual letter.

Disputing false information can get a lot of accounts dropped and it can remove some of your debt because you won't have to pay for those collections or past due charges if you can prove that they are not accurate. Plus, this is going to improve your credit score and repair your credit because the negative accounts are being removed.

You could be 100% right in your disputes and the collection agency could be wrong, but for some reason you will still be met with resistance because of the structure of the credit system as a whole. Many people who have come to me with stories of them negotiating with a collection agency or a creditor not knowing the rules to the game. People have high hopes of finally getting their credit in order and they truly have good intentions, but they are met with false promises from these debt collectors who are only after their money. For some reason even after all these years; people are still under the impression that just because they pay a collection or charge-off account it will result in the derogatory item being removed from their credit, they couldn't be more wrong. No collection agency will tell you this upfront, their job isn't to help you, it is to secure a payment and collect a debt by any means necessary. If you choose not to fight, or don't have the patience, I suggest any negotiations for you to pay for a deletion should always show your agreement 100% in writing.

Write letters to the agencies with the correct but bad items you have encountered and your reasoning for which you think they should be taken off your credit report. The most important thing when writing these letters and when making any type of contact with the people at the credit report agencies is to keep communication very polite and professional. The more pleasant and prepared you are, the more you increase the chances of them helping you repair your credit. Sign and date your letters and try to write them by hand. If you have no experience with writing business letters or don't think your handwriting will be of much help, try to find templates for the type of business letter you need. The Internet is filled with appropriate templates and all you have to do is fill in information like your name and problem, without having to worry about proper business language.

The reason for which I suggested you send your letter with the additional costs of certified mail is that so you know exactly when your letter has reached its destination. It is extremely important to be aware of this, because the law stipulates that the agencies have to verify whatever claims you make and respond to you after a reasonable time of usually thirty days. This law is well known by everyone working in credit report agencies, which is why they will proceed to check your credit report immediately because if not, the item you contested becomes unverifiable and will be removed by default. If you see the customary period of time has passed, write another letter reminding the agency to remove the contested entry, in accordance with the law.

Don't cram all the problems you've encountered into a single letter, as that will unnecessarily encumber the employee working on fixing your credit reports and if they are stressed a decision in your favor will be harder to reach. Keep it about two or three issues per letter and, if you think you are concise and specific in your requests, maybe add a few more. It all really depends on what the problems you've encountered contain and how you have formulated your reasoning. If you send a letter and it has a huge number of problems you've considered wrong, they might categorize your claims as frivolous. The law permits credit reporting agencies to discard "frivolous requests" so be careful how many issues per letter you dispute and how you express yourself in your letter. Just state who you are and what you think the problem is, that you have a right to have your claims investigated and that you are happy to help the agency with all the information they require. Professionalism and politeness will go a long way. If you think it will be best to send more letters, try to send them a few days apart from each other, so that the people working at the agency have more time to investigate each claim in an adequate way.

After you send your first letter, the process of reviewing your credit report begins. As you probably know, the negative information you've submitted may actually be accurate and the reply to your letter might say that they've investigated your claim and they can't remove the item from your credit report. If you want to keep pressing the issue, write a second letter including all the information from the letter and request further verifications as well as the contact information of the employees that were responsible at the creditor company. Usually they will have no problem with giving you the contact information of the person at the creditor firm, so now you can discuss directly with them about the problem and possibly begin a negotiation on the matter.

If you've cleared some issues from your credit report, you can consider the first steps towards repairing your credit to be successful. Chances are that, after correcting some errors and trying to get the problems removed by default or re-evaluated, you'll still be left with problems. These are the most difficult to remove as they are accurate and legitimate fiscal missteps that you've taken at one point. This is why you should directly contact the person at the creditor office, as these kinds of problems can only be removed from your credit report through extensive negotiations, which will now begin.

Even if you know that you can repair your credit, don't just jump into it without coming up with a strategy. The first thing you should do is to list all the accounts you intend to dispute then follow with sending dispute letters for each of the accounts. You can use any of the three methods:

- Send the dispute letters through email
- Visit the individual credit bureau's office then file the dispute
- File the dispute online

Don't aim to have zero balances for accounts that you settle. Instead, you should have them removed completely because a zero balance taints your rating. This zero balance will show in your report for 7 years or more; it speaks that creditors should take caution when dealing with you. You don't want that! You would rather fail to pay the debt to let it expire instead of having your credit score tainted by the derogatory zero balance! As such, even if you are to go into a pay to delete arrangement with a creditor. So, what should you have in your dispute letters?

- Your Last and First name (must be spelled correctly)
- Your SSN
- Your Driver's license
- Your current home address
- Your W2 form or pay stub showing your name and SSN
- Your first and last name spelled accurately
- Any other forms of identification you may have

If you don't correct all these mistakes your dispute will not be accepted, it's also important to note that all the necessary information in the dispute. Look out for variations in account numbers for the same account as creditors could sometimes have different numbers for different bureaus.

1. Credit Mistakes

When it comes to credit reports there is one thing that should be taken into consideration. What should be understood is that mistakes happen. These mistakes are not "mistakes" in the sense of some irresponsible action on the part of the consumer or anything of a similar nature. Instead these mistakes are actually errors that appear on a credit report. The erroneous information on the credit report could be reported incorrectly, belong to some other person, or even be against the law.

The fact that these errors can occur is a reason why it is important for a person to check their credit report. According to the Federal Trade Commission 25% of Americans have at least one major error in their credit reports. These errors are causing the millions of people to have worse credit than they actually have, which means that they are paying more for things that they are supposed to pay. This causes the snowball effect where they incur more debts, higher fees, and even loss of financial opportunities all through no fault of their own. In short, credit mistakes are dangerous.

In order to avoid the path of financial danger a person should carefully look over their credit report to spot errors that could actually be hurting their credit. Thankfully many of the errors are easy to spot and can be reported in order to repair the damage done. The most common credit report errors fall under three categories: personal information errors, account related errors, and derogatory mark errors.

Derogatory marks are long lasting negative records on a credit report. These marks generally last for at least 7 years on a credit report and have a huge ability to hurt a person's credit. Bankruptcy, tax liens, collections, and foreclosures are examples of derogatory marks. Because of the severity of damage derogatory marks can cause errors of this sort are especially dangerous.

There are a few key things to look for when it comes to derogatory mark errors. One such error to be wary of is a collections account that has been paid off still remaining on the credit report as unpaid. This is an obvious error that is easy to dispute. There will be documentation showing that the account has been paid and contacting the creditor directly often leads to satisfactory results in getting the issue resolved.

Another common derogatory mark error is a paid tax lien that has remained on a credit report for more than 7 years after the last date of payment. While an unpaid tax lien may stay on a credit report indefinitely, there is simply no reason for a tax lien that has been paid to remain after 7 years. It is a black mark on a credit report that does not need to exist.

A discharged account displayed as an active balance is also a key error to keep an eye on. This is perhaps the most damaging of derogatory marks because it concerns bankruptcy. A person files for bankruptcy as a last resort in order to gain some relief from debt obligations. The individual has entered into a legal process in an attempt to address overwhelming debt. Bankruptcy changes the accounts a person holds and the person no longer has the same active balances they had before filing for bankruptcy. Therefore, when a discharged account appears on a credit report as active what this does to a person's credit is damage it even further than is legally allowed. The bankrupt accounts are already in a special legal process to prevent further debts and that means it is close to impossible to actually have an active account with a balance.

These derogatory mark errors should be immediately disputed in order to prevent any further damage to one's credit. While all credit errors should be disputed, it is the derogatory marks that are the most damaging due to the sheer amount of time they remain on a credit report and the severity of the impact they can incur on an individual.

A person that erroneously has an unpaid tax lien on their credit report could potentially be feeling the financial effect of that mistake for life simply because they didn't look at their credit report and dispute the mistake. The other common types of errors should not be discounted however.

Account related errors are mistakes that occur which are still damaging but not to the same severity as derogatory marks. These are errors tend to be simple fixes that take little effort to correct and probably only occur as an oversight.

An example of an account related error is a late payment that has remained on the credit report after 7 years. Generally, a credit report only lists negative information on an account for 7 years, after which it is removed from the credit report. It should be noted that the debt negative items cause still exist and still impact a person's credit. However, after the allotted time they can no longer incur more of an effect, in other words the 7-year mark is the ceiling for damage to a credit report. When a late payment remains on a credit report after this time that means it is still causing a negative impact on a person's credit. This should not appear on a credit report and should be disputed.

Another common account related error is one that is more the result of simple human error, however it could still have a negative impact if left undisputed. A loan or credit card listed on a credit report that does not belong to the individual is an error that happens on a regular basis. There could be any number of reasons for these to appear but usually it is the result of a person that had a simple mix-up while entering data. The worst-case scenario is actually a more frightening occurrence because the erroneous accounts could be the result of fraud or identity theft.

The first thing to do in either scenario is for the individual to report the false accounts directly to the credit bureau which lists the accounts. This can be done by mail, fax, email, or over the phone. It is quicker to do it by phone however disputing the account by mail provides a paper trail that can be used to support the claim that the person is actively trying to dispute the false accounts. Whichever method is chosen the following step should be to close the damaging account to prevent any future harm. Thankfully the process of fixing this error often proves successful and the fraudulent or erroneous account will be removed efficiently from the credit report.

The final category of credit mistakes is erroneous personal information. This category is the least damaging of mistakes but still has an effect on a person's credit. Like account related errors, these mistakes can often simply be attributed to human error. Thankfully personal information mistakes are the easiest to fix due to them not being directly related to financial actions.

The most common error when it comes to personal information is simply having the wrong name listed. This could be as harmless as spelling a person's name incorrectly or using an individual's maiden name after they've married. Another common error is a wrong mailing address listed on a credit report. Perhaps a person with a similar name lived at the mistaken address and whomever is responsible for correcting that information simply overlooked it. This could also happen when a person's employer information is displayed inaccurately on a credit report, a person with a similar name may have been employed by the mistaken employer.

Generally, mistakes in personal information have little to no effect on an individual's credit score. Unless the error is related to something along the lines of fraud or identity theft then there is no reason to be worried. Simply reporting to the creditors the mistake in personal information is enough to fix the problem and no harm would be done to the person's credit.

When these mistakes are made they can be removed from a person's credit report. These items are also automatically removed after the regulatory 7 years have passed, generally. However, it is also possible to remove all negative items from a credit report. The process is not difficult and can go a long way towards improving a person's credit standing.

One of the most surprising and efficient ways to remove a negative item such as a late payment is to write a letter. Often called a goodwill letter or goodwill adjustment, a person can write (or call, although writing is better) to a creditor to get a late payment forgiven and thus removed from a credit report. This tends to work best if a person has a good history with the creditor as that makes them more likely to forgive the late payment as a one-time issue.

When contacting the creditor a few key things must be discussed with them for the best results. First of all, an explanation is owed to the creditor for the late payment. Telling the creditor the financial situation that led to the payment being late could generate some understanding and sympathy. People are not perfect and unexpected events do occur, after all. Creditors are not machines but are institutions ran by people who can relate to what another person is going through.

What should also be discussed with the creditor is an explanation of the history with the creditor. A person that reminds the creditor that they have been in great standing with no issue can reinforce the fact that the late payment was not a regular occurrence. Requesting the removal of the negative mark should be made only after it has been established that there will be no repeat of late payments.

This tactic of writing the creditor to remove the late payment from a credit report is often more successful than people would imagine. Creditors are always willing to negotiate with people because they want their business. It should be noted that writing the creditor to request the removal of a late payment only works for those who are in good standing with the creditor. A person with a history of late payments is far less likely to get a sympathetic response as they have not shown that they are trust worthy. However even in that scenario it is still very likely that the creditor would be willing to negotiate a payment plan at the very least.

Regardless of the one's standing with a creditor it is always a helpful and beneficial plan to contact them. If a person is not able to remove the negative marks from their credit report then they are still going to be able to discuss options that will lead to positive impacts to a credit score in the future.

That is the biggest secret to getting negative items removed from a credit report, simply contacting the creditor. Many people are afraid of doing so because they feel that it would be difficult or they simply want to avoid the confrontation, but it cannot be stressed enough that a creditor is always willing to negotiate. Combining this with the fact that the passage of time can generally takes care of negative marks on a credit report and that leaves a clean credit report. In conjunction with a person checking their credit report for mistakes and monitoring changes results in a credit report that will remain free of negative marks for as long as the individual continues to be responsible.

Credit mistakes are common, that much is clear. With the proper tools and understanding is far easier than people realize to fix these errors, especially since these errors are not the result of negligent or poor behavior on the part of the individual but rather that of the financial institutions, creditors, and bureaus. Mistakes happen, that much is unavoidable. What should be done to fix these mistakes, regardless of who is at fault, is swift and steady action on the part of the wronged person. There is simply no reason or benefit to walking around with a debt on a person's record that should not be there. Nor is there any reason to ignore their credit report and the mistakes listed on them. Vigilance is a requirement in order to make sure one's credit standing is as accurate as possible. Bureaus and other financial institutions are run by humans, not machines, so mistakes should be expected. Again, staying vigilant is the key.

1. Your Financial Freedom

Financial freedom is a concept that people love to think about but rarely feel like they can reach. This chapter will help you reach financial freedom by using tips and habits that can be incorporated into your life.

What Is Meant by Financial Freedom?

Financial freedom has no set definition. However, it typically means that you are living comfortably and saving for retirement and in general. It can also mean that you have an emergency reserve set up. In general, financial freedom can mean whatever you want it to mean for you. For example, a prior college student may not think that financial freedom includes paying off all their student loans. This is because, at least in this day and age, a college student who needs to pay their own way realizes they will always be paying off their student loans. However, they might feel that student loans are the only debt they should have. Therefore, being able to pay off credit cards or medical bills leads them to financial freedom.

Some people might feel that financial freedom indicates they have absolutely no debt or loans. This includes them having paid off their mortgage and any car loans. They might also feel that in order to reach financial freedom, they need to be investing in a CD, bond, or even in the stock market.

Other people may feel that financial freedom means they are no longer tied down to a job. They are able to live off of their savings or a passive income, and they are able to retire and enjoy life through traveling.

Credit Cards and Financial Freedom - Is It Safe?

One of the biggest questions people have when it comes to financial freedom is whether they can have any credit card accounts in their name. While you may not owe anything on your credit cards (in fact, you might only owe one which you pay off in full every month), is this still financial freedom? In general, this is completely determined by your definition of financial freedom. However, if you ever find yourself not being able to pay off your credit card every month, this is not financial freedom. In most cases, financial freedom does mean you no longer have any debt, or at least that you are free from unnecessary debt, such as credit cards.

Most people are quick to state that financial freedom and credit cards do not go together simply because they are not safe with each other. This is due to the fact that it is often easy to fall back into thinking you can pay the amount off everything each month and then you become unable to do so. In general, people who reach financial freedom feel that credit cards allow for more of a trap and keep them from ever reaching financial freedom.

However, other people who feel they have reached financial freedom state that as long as you can manage your credit cards wisely, they can be included with your freedom. Some of them also advise that you set up a financial freedom plan. Within this plan, you will state your conditions of using a credit card. Of course, you need to be self-disciplined enough to follow your condition.

The Best Habits to Help You Reach and Protect Your Financial Freedom

When it comes to financial freedom, there are dozens of habits and tips that people provide in order to help you reach your financial freedom. It is important to note that because financial freedom can vary depending on the person's definition, some of the tips and habits might work for you while others may not. You need to find the ones that work best for you, not the ones that other people say are the best. Therefore, I am going to give you a fairly large list as I want you to make sure that you can find some of the best habits and tips so you can not only reach financial freedom but also protect it.

Make a Budget

Making and keeping a budget is one of the first steps everyone should take while heading towards your financial freedom. Even though you might find yourself changing your budget now and then, as you will add or delete bills or receive a different income, you always want to follow it. Not only will this help you in reaching your financial freedom, but continuing to follow your budget will also protect your financial freedom.

Furthermore, creating a monthly budget can make sure that all your bills are being paid and you know exactly where your money is going. For example, you will be able to see how much money you spend on groceries, gas, and eating out at restaurants. This will help you know where you can decrease your spending, which will allow you to save more. There are a lot of great benefits when it comes to creating and sticking with a household budget.

Set Up Automatic Savings Account

If you work for an organization that will automatically place a certain percentage of your check into a savings account, take advantage of this. It gives you the idea that you never had the money to begin with, which means you don't plan for it and you won't find yourself taking the money out of savings unless you need it for an emergency. Furthermore, you can set up a separate savings account where this money will go. You can make it so you rarely see this account, however, you want to make sure that your money is deposited and everything looks right on your account. But, the point of this account if you do not touch it, even if you have an emergency. Instead, you will set up a different account for emergency basis.

The other idea to this is you pay yourself first. This is often something that people don't think about because they are more worried about paying off their debt. However, many financial advisors say that you are always number one when it comes to your finances. While you want to pay your bills, you also need to make sure that you and your family are taken care of.

Keep Your Credit in Mind Without Obsessing Over It

Your credit score is important, but it is not the most important thing in the world. People often fall into the trap of becoming obsessed over their credit score, especially when they are trying to improve it. One factor to remember is that your credit score is typically only updated every so often. Therefore, you can decide to set time aside every quarter to check on your credit report. When you do this, you not only want to check your score, but you also want to check what the credit bureaus are reporting. Just like you want to make sure everything is correct on your bank account, you want to do the same thing for your credit report.

It Is Fine to Live Below Your Means

One of the biggest factors of financial freedom and being able to maintain it is you can make your bills and comfortably live throughout the month. In order to do this, you need to make sure that the money coming into your home is more than the money going out. In other words, you want to live below your means.

This is often difficult for a lot of people because they want to have what other people have. They want to have the newer vehicles, the bigger boat, the newest grill, or anything else. People like to have what their friends and neighbors have. However, one-factor people don't think about is that their friends and neighbors probably don't have financial freedom. Therefore, you want to take a moment to think about what is more important for you. Would you rather be in debt like your friends or you would rather have financial freedom?

Speak With a Financial Advisor

Sometimes the best steps we can take when we are working towards financial freedom is to talk with a financial advisor. They can often give up information and help us with a budget, ways to make sure that we get the most out of our income, and also tell us where we might be spending more money than we should. Furthermore, they can help you figure out what the best investments are, which are always helpful when you are looking at financial freedom. At the same time, they can help you plan for your retirement, which is one of the biggest ways you will be able to remain financially free.

Completely Pay Off Your Credit Cards

If you are high-interest credit cards, which is often the case, you want to make sure that you pay these off every month. Therefore, your credit card spending should become part of your budget. What this means is you don't want to use your credit card for whatever you feel like. Instead, you want to create a list on when you can and when you can't use your credit card. For example, you might agree that it is fine in emergency situations or during Christmas shopping. You might also feel that you can use it during tips because it has trip insurance attached to it. Whatever you decide, you want to make sure you follow.

You also want to make sure that you pay off any high-interest loans. When it comes to loans that are lower in interest, they won't affect you too much.

Track Your Spending

Along with making sure you follow your budget, you also want to track your spending. There are several reasons for this. First, it will help you make sure that your budget is on track. We often forget about automatic bills that are paid monthly or don't realize how much we really spend every month. These factors can make our budget off, which can cause an obstacle when you are working to reaching and keeping your financial freedom.

Fortunately, there are a lot of apps that you can download, many of them are free, which will allow you to easily track your spending. Some of these apps include Mint or Personal Capital. These apps typically give you all the information you need and will automatically tell you how much you are spending and how much income you still hold at the end of the month. Most of these apps will also give you charts to help you see your spending habits in a different way.

Continue Your Education

Another way to stay on top of your financial freedom is to become educated when it comes to your budget, spending, taxes, and anything else to do with your finances. This doesn't mean that you have to go back to school and earn a degree. You can simply do your own research or take online classes, some of which you will find are low-cost to free. You can also look into webinars that people hold.

You can also help yourself when it comes to investing in the stock market or anything else. There are always several classes you can take online which only have a few sessions or ways you can learn when you have the time. In fact, if you want to invest but don't know what to do or where to begin, one of your best options is to take a class.

Make Sure to Keep Your Mindset

This is a mindset that you will want to continue to have while you are living financially free. With this mindset, you will not only feel grateful for where you are in life, but you will also remember where you once were. This will help you work towards protecting your financial freedom instead of falling back into credit card debt.

Of course, you can adjust your mindset the way you want to once you reach financial freedom. However, you will want to make sure that you keep your mindset positive. After all, a positive mindset makes you believe that you can accomplish anything.

Make Sure You Write down What Financial Freedom Means to You

As stated before, financial freedom can mean something different to you than it means to someone else. Because of this, you have to think about what it truly means to you. Whatever you feel it means, it is important to write this down. This will allow you to turn back to what financial freedom means to you when you find yourself struggling and feeling like you can't gain your financial freedom.

At the same time, it is also helpful to take time to write down your goals. Think of what you want to accomplish on your road to financial freedom. You can also think about what you want to do after you have reached financial freedom. Give yourself goals to work towards as this will help you stay on track better.

Conclusion

Your credit score might seem like a small number, but it is incredibly powerful. Various businesses and financial institutions often use your credit score. It can influence your daily life in ways you might have never imagined. From the rates of interest payable to the ease with which you can get a new credit card, everything is based on your credit score. So, by repairing your credit score, you can improve your financial health. Remember that it isn't about just repairing your credit score, but must also maintain the same.

As promised, you were given various practical strategies as well as tips you can use to improve your credit score. It will do you good to remember that you cannot improve your credit score overnight and it takes a lot of effort. Trust me; it is better to put in the necessary effort to improve your credit score because it will change your life. Mindful spending habits, patience, and consistent effort are required. When it comes to your life, there are many things that you can control, but your credit score can be entirely regulated by you. If you keep your wits about you, then maintaining a good credit score is easy.

Now, all that's left to do is to get started and implement various practical tips given in this book. If you found this book useful in anyway then please leave a review on Amazon. It would be greatly appreciated!

Thank you and all the best!

www.ingramcontent.com/pod-product-compliance
Lightning Source LLC
LaVergne TN
LVHW090425210926
848480LV00002B/683
* 9 7 9 8 2 0 1 4 8 3 8 1 4 *